THE World Crisis
THE WAY FORWARD AFTER IRAQ

With a Foreword by
Geoffrey Howe

Edited and Introduced by
Robert Harvey

Constable · London

Constable & Robinson Ltd
3 The Lanchesters
161 Fulham Palace Road
London W6 9ER

www.constablerobinson.com

First published by Constable,
an imprint of Constable & Robinson Ltd, 2008

For a full list of contributors and individual copyright details,
please see pages iii–iv

A copy of the British Library Cataloguing in Publication data is
available from the British Library

ISBN: 978-1-84529-870-8

Printed and bound in the EU
1 3 5 7 9 10 8 6 4 2

Foreword: 'Towards a Safer World'
© Geoffrey Howe, 2008

Introduction: 'The World Century'
© Robert Harvey, 2008

'Reclaiming the Values of the United States'
© Jimmy Carter, 2008

'The Post-Westphalian World'
© Henry A. Kissinger, 2008

'Protecting the Golden Moment'
© George P. Shultz, Harry Rowen, 2008

'British Foreign Policy: the Folly of Iraq'
© Geoffrey Howe, 2008

'Doing Our Fighting Men and Women Justice'
© Michael Heseltine, 2008

'Uniting Our Enemies and Dividing Our Friends'
© Dr Zbigniew Brzezinski, 2008

'Traditionalists vs. Transformationists'
© Brent Scowcroft, 2008

'The United States Cannot Stand Alone'
© Frank Carlucci, 2008

'The Bridge of Dreams'
© David Howell, 2008

'Forging Nuclear Warheads into Lightbulbs'
© Sam Nunn, 2008

'The Challenge of Energy Security'
© Dick G. Lugar, 2008

'Who Will *Do* Foreign Policy?'
© Sir John Coles, 2008

CONTENTS

Each of the authors is responsible only for the views expressed in their own articles; their inclusion in this book does not necessarily imply agreement with any of the other articles, although obviously there are many common views and threads.

LIST OF CONTRIBUTORS

Sir Mark Allen is a retired member of HM Diplomatic Service.

The Hon. Dr Zbigniew Brzezinski is a former National Security Adviser to President Carter, counsellor for the Centre of Strategic and International Studies and Professor at Nitze School for Advanced International Studies at Johns Hopkins University.

The Hon. Frank C. Carlucci is a former US Secretary of Defense and former National Security Advisor to the President.

The Hon. Jimmy Carter was the 39th President of the United States. A former governor of Georgia, he is founder of the Carter Center, the author of numerous books and a winner of the Nobel Peace Prize.

Sir John Coles is the former head of the British Diplomatic Service.

The Hon. Chas W. Freeman, Jr. is a former US Ambassador to Saudi Arabia and to China.

Robert Harvey is a former MP and member of the House of Commons Foreign Affairs Committee, former Assistant Editor of the *Economist*, former editorialist on the *Daily Telegraph* and the author of *Global Disorder*.

The Rt. Hon. Michael Heseltine (Lord Heseltine of Thenford) is a former British Secretary of State for the Environment, Secretary of State for Defence, Secretary of State for Trade and Industry and Deputy Prime Minister.

Professor Sir Michael Howard is the former Regius Professor of History at Oxford.

The Rt. Hon. Geoffrey Howe (Lord Howe of Aberavon) is a former British Chancellor of the Exchequer, Foreign Secretary and Deputy Prime Minister.

The Rt. Hon. David Howell (Lord Howell of Guildford) is a former British Secretary of State for Energy and is currently Deputy Leader of the Conservative Party in the House of Lords.

Simon Jenkins is a columnist on the *Guardian* and the *Sunday Times* and a former Editor of *The Times*.

The Hon. Henry A. Kissinger is a former United States Secretary of State and National Security Advisor to the President. He is President of Kissinger Associates and a winner of the Nobel Peace Prize.

Senator Dick Lugar is a former Republican Chairman of the Senate Foreign Relations Committee.

Senator Sam Nunn is a former Democratic Chairman of the Senate Armed Forces Committee.

Simon Scott Plummer is former chief foreign affairs editorialist on the London *Daily Telegraph* and former Diplomatic Editor of the *Daily Telegraph* and *The Times*.

The Hon. Harry Rowen is a former Assistant Secretary of Defense and Senior Fellow at the Hoover Institution, Stanford University.

The Hon. George P. Shultz is a former US Secretary of State, Secretary of the Treasury, Secretary of Labor and Professor Emeritus at Stanford.

The Hon. Brent Scowcroft, Lt-General US Army (retired) is a former National Security Advisor to President George H.W. Bush.

The Hon. Branko Terzic is Global Regulatory Policy Leader for Energy and Resources in Deloitte Services LP, Chairman of the UN ECE Ad Hoc Group of Experts on Cleaner Electricity Production from Coal and other Fossil Fuels, and a former director of the US National Grid.

ACKNOWLEDGEMENTS

I owe immense thanks to the four principal co-architects of this book: Lord Richard Ryder, whose idea it was and whose wise advice and help throughout has been invaluable; Lord Geoffrey Howe, who secured the participation of so many of the contributors, for his own contributions and whose razor-sharp mind has helped to finesse so many judgements in the book; the Hon. Ed Streator, who has tirelessly worked to help obtain so many distinguished contributors from the United States and offered many perceptive judgements as well; and my assistant Jenny Thomas, a skilful editor herself, who has worked tirelessly, as always, to meet my unreasonable demands and deadlines.

I also wish warmly to thank the following for their co-operation and help: The Ditchley Foundation; the Nuclear Threat Initiative and The Globalisation Institute.

I also owe a huge debt of gratitude to Andrew Williams and Economic and Political Research Ltd., who helped with the publication of this book, to my inspired publishers Nick Robinson and Leo Hollis, to my brilliant agent and friend, Gillon Aitken, for his advice, and to my mother Jane and Oliver, who put up with it all.

Robert Harvey, 2008

FOREWORD: TOWARDS A SAFER WORLD

Geoffrey Howe

This book brings together perhaps the most senior grouping of American and British statesmen ever assembled under one roof, expressing for the first time their candid and strongly felt opinions about the disturbing trend of world events. I asked them to contribute, and am enormously grateful for their response.

These are historic American names – Carter, Shultz, Kissinger, Brzezinski, Carlucci, Scowcroft, Nunn and Lugar, along with many others from both parties – and the verdict is clear: we got it wrong over the past eight years, let's get it right in time for a presidency that returns America to its traditional values of peace reaching out to all nations and using force as a very last resort. The British contributions point in exactly the same direction.

The book is in large part a repudiation of the international policies of the past eight years which, however well intentioned, were the most aberrant and naive in recent American and British history, legitimizing unprovoked wars that caused the unnecessary deaths of tens of thousands of civilians and thousands of brave servicemen and women, departing from previous constraints, eschewing diplomacy for force with disastrous short- and long-term results. Thankfully these years are almost past us; they risked turning the West into the villains of international politics.

The views expressed here are all the more effective for being written in statesmanlike, gentle, restrained, carefully argued and measured terms. Above all they are constructive, a manifesto of recommendations. For they are not being voiced by the usual anti-American left, or even liberals: they are written by former senior public servants, Republican, Democrat and some of their British counterparts, many of them directly involved with bringing to an end the Cold War.

Indeed, for many years now I have been increasingly dismayed by the turn that international relations are taking. Instead of building upon the huge achievement of the end of the Cold War, too many in the West have become obsessed with far lesser threats (mostly Middle East-based and exemplified by the horrific tragedy of 9/11), exaggerating them out of all proportion and thereby magnifying dangers which had previously been more or less containable, specifically in Iraq and Afghanistan. As two former Presidential National Security Advisors, Henry Kissinger and Zbigniew Brzezinski, remind us here, those were the days in which at the press of a button tens of millions could have been annihilated by nuclear war. While today's security threats remain extremely serious, and certainly must be addressed, they cannot credibly match that order of magnitude. Today's so-called 'war on terror' so far bears little comparison with either of the two world wars or with the Cold War itself. As the United Kingdom's Foreign Secretary alongside Margaret Thatcher, when we welcomed Mikhail Gorbachev on his first crucial visit to the West, I can testify that the atmosphere then was dramatically darker than ever it is today.

Working together with a former US Ambassador to the OECD Edward Streator, and two British colleagues, Richard

Ryder and Robert Harvey, I invited senior policymakers from both sides of the Atlantic to contribute their thoughts to a short book, with practical recommendations on how to break out of this slough of despair and grasp the great opportunities presented by the twenty-first century – probably the most exciting yet in the history of mankind. The eagerness of their response and the passion of their views reflects the critical juncture we are at in history.

All of these 'Twenty Wise Men' have immense experience. They include a former Democratic US President; two former Republican Secretaries of State; two former British Deputy Prime Ministers (one of them – myself – a former Foreign Secretary, the other a former Defence Secretary); a former British Energy Secretary; four former National Security Advisors to the President (one Democrat, three Republican); a Republican former US Secretary of Defense; a former Republican Chairman of the US Senate Foreign Relations Committee; a former Democrat Chairman of the US Senate Armed Services Committee; a former Assistant US Defense Secretary; a former US Ambassador to China and Saudi Arabia; a former head of the British Foreign Office; a former head of the US National Grid and current Chairman of the UN's Clean Energy Committee; a former deputy head of MI6; the United Kingdom's most distinguished academic defence expert; a former member of the House of Commons Foreign Affairs Committee; and two eminent British journalists.

Even more important than their combined experience has been their ability, as figures above the fray, to speak freely, freed from the constraints of office or fear of prejudicing their careers. These are entirely dispassionate opinions from some of the most eminent names in the fields of foreign affairs and defence to have been brought together in recent years. The idea was to provide a contribution to the debate well in time for consideration by the upcoming US administrations – whichever party takes office in 2009. We do not share the view that the next US government will simply continue the policies of the current one. On the contrary, the policies of one administration have frequently been reversed by the next. The US is a vibrant society, and capable of learning from its mistakes.

Sadly, contributions from other countries could not be brought into the dialogue for it would then have been spread too thinly. Links between the United Kingdom and the United States are sufficiently significant in themselves – not least in their role in bringing the US and Europe closer together – that we felt our recommendations at this stage would have a more useful impact if they were limited to the two nations. Hopefully it will be possible to continue and expand the dialogue later on.

The truly remarkable thing about these essays – from Americans who served at the very highest level, both Republicans and Democrats, as well as their British counterparts – is the breadth of their consensus on what needs to be done. These are not sterile analyses of the mistakes of the past, but forward-looking, practical recommendations, a real blueprint for action which tackles immediate challenges with resolve and looks forward with optimism to a future of unprecedented opportunity and self-fulfilment for not just a few, mainly in the developed nations, but the great majority of peoples around the world. While the view of each contributor is entirely his own and represents no endorsement of any other, I would suggest there is remarkable agreement among most (not all) on the following points:

1. The coalition invasion of Iraq, however well-intentioned its promoters might proclaim it, has been beyond doubt a disaster (see the essays by Carter, Howe, Heseltine, Brzezinski, Freeman, Howard, Jenkins and Harvey), and there are increasing doubts about whether the intervention in Afghanistan, while originally justified by the 9/11 attacks, makes sense (Heseltine, Jenkins, Harvey).

2. The US should commit itself to a much more multilateralist approach, exerting diplomatic and economic pressure and resorting to force, if at all, only as a very last resort (Carter, Kissinger, Howe, Heseltine, Brzezinski, Scowcroft, Carlucci, Howard, Harvey).

3. Terrorism, while a very serious challenge, is not remotely comparable to the wars between major states of the last century, which ultimately threatened nuclear annihilation (Kissinger, Brzezinski, Scowcroft, Howard). The threat does not justify an official culture of scaremongering, much less the erosion of the civil liberties that are the foundations of western societies and which have survived much more dangerous challenges (Carter, Jenkins, Harvey).

4. Today's biggest security threat probably stems from the threat of nuclear proliferation, nuclear stockpiles (still on alert) and the related possibility that terrorist groups might acquire a nuclear weapon or 'dirty bomb'. No country can completely insulate itself against this hazard, but the prospect can – and must – be substantially reduced by a much more consistently rigorous non-proliferation regime (Carter, Kissinger, Shultz, Rowen, Brzezinski, Scowcroft, Nunn).

5. There is a major need for the United States and Russia to slash their still large stockpiles of nuclear weapons, even perhaps with a view to their eventual elimination, as a trade-off for global acceptance of a non-proliferation regime (Carter, Shultz, Rowen, Nunn).

6. The issue of reform of successful Cold War institutions in need of improvement such as the UN and NATO needs to be addressed urgently to reflect the reality of a very different world, in which the generation of economic growth may be decisively tilted towards Asia and the new 'great powers'. A more consensual and effective international security structure needs to be put in place (Shultz, Brzezinski, Scowcroft, Howell, Howard, Harvey).

7. The United States and its allies must continue to pursue the goal of averting humanitarian catastrophes, and promoting freedom and democracy. But except in extraordinary circumstances this needs to be done through economic and diplomatic leverage, and very rarely by force. Different societies at different stages of development cannot be turned into democracies overnight without risking immense suffering of the kind experienced in Iraq. This is not cynical 'realpolitik'; it is humanity and commonsense (Carter, Howe, Kissinger, Howard, Allen).

8. The United States and the European Union should reconcile themselves to the emergence of major new powers around the world – China, India, Japan, Brazil and Mexico, and one day South Africa and Nigeria. The US remains overwhelmingly the strongest military power, but cannot compel others to do its bidding. However, it can persuade and lead through force of example (Kissinger, Carlucci, Howe, Heseltine, Brzezinski, Scowcroft, Freeman, Howard, Harvey).

9. Good US–EU relations ('a grand consensus', in Brzezinski's words) are absolutely key to global security and prosperity (Kissinger, Shultz, Rowen, Howe, Heseltine, Brzezinski, Scowcroft, Harvey). The US is right to press for a greater European commitment to security, and a more united and coherent foreign policy voice and role for the European Union, which shares a common heritage and democratic value. But not every British contributor shares this view. However, there is a British consensus that the Commonwealth has a major role to play (Howe, Howell).

10. The US and Europe must at last recognize the need for far stronger and indefinitely sustained efforts to find a satisfactory settlement of the Israel–Palestinian conflict (Carter, Howe, Brzezinski), if necessary with US and European forces as its guarantor.

11. Russia needs to be 'neither isolated nor propitiated', as Brzezinski says, but drawn ever more closely into the western economic and political community (Kissinger, Shultz, Rowan, Brzezinski, Scowcroft, Nunn).

12. A world in which there is an ever-greater demand for energy, particularly among newly emerging powers, must address the issue of security of energy supplies and fair pricing as a priority (Lugar, Terzic, Howell).

13. Global warming should be treated as a pressing global concern. Measures should be undertaken on an effective worldwide basis (not limited to a few selective western countries), while showing awareness of the need to improve living standards in developing countries. Solutions should encourage global economic growth and should be carefully considered in the light of clear scientific evidence (Shultz, Rowen, Terzic, Scott Plummer), also being targeted at the consequences of global warming (Howell).

14. The global economy has already provided huge increases in living standards across the world, and has the potential to provide much more. The danger that large parts of these are being left behind and that inequalities between, and within, nations which could create a backlash are rapidly increasing. This needs to be addressed both at national and international level (Kissinger, Shultz, Rowen, Brzezinski, Scowcroft).

15. Modern means of communication, in particular the internet, mobile telephones and television, provide a new 'political globalization' in which educated or like-minded people across the globe can make common cause in communicating their views across thousands of miles. The global environmental movement, anti-globalization movements and, in extreme form, Islamic terrorism, are manifestations. Global political organizations may not be far over the horizon (Brzezinski, Howell).

16. The United Kingdom needs to return to long-established traditions of cabinet and parliamentary government, and

to restore, enhance and exploit the long-respected expertise of its diplomatic service and well-trained and professional armed forces (Howe, Heseltine, Howard, Coles, Harvey).

These are the main issues addressed in this book which, as I say, points a clear way forward out of the street-level gloom that seems, mostly unnecessarily, to have engulfed many western governments, policymakers and commentators as we embark upon this most exciting of centuries. The arguments are clearly, honestly and I hope readably presented, and the practical recommendations positive and constructive (see in particular Shultz, Rowen and Nunn on nuclear weaponry, Lugar on energy security, Terzic on energy-saving, Scowcroft and Harvey on reforming international institutions and, in a significantly British context, Heseltine on defence and Coles on the Foreign Office). This analysis and these recommendations do, I believe, offer a way forward towards a safer world.

INTRODUCTION: THE WORLD CENTURY

Robert Harvey

The twenty-first century will not be an American, European or even an Asian century. It will be the World Century. The globe is bound together by instant communications, common problems and a proliferation of new 'Great Powers'. Collectively we face the immensely exciting possibility of billions of people being raised from no-hope destitution and poverty to fulfilling, meaningful and increasingly prosperous lives undreamt of by their parents. Within a single generation, China and India have become giant economic powerhouses, drawing hundreds of millions out of a subsistence existence. Other Asian countries – Indonesia, Malaysia, Thailand, Vietnam – are emulating the 'tiger economies' and are also developing quickly.

Eastern Europe is racing ahead of its old hegemon, Russia (now sinking into a petrodollar sludge), in creating economically-dynamic, politically-pluralist societies, even though much of it is still hindered by deep inequality, corruption, bureaucratic inertia and regional fragmentation. Latin America, led by Brazil, is developing at a steady pace. Even Africa, in some instances, is shedding its band-aid, basket-case, 'Big Man' caricatures and incubating a handful of democratic seeds alongside some of the fastest growing economies in the world. Only the wider Middle East remains mired in national and sectarian strife, a product of its immense history combined with the corrupting and narcotic effects of oil wealth – and even that generalization masks huge differences between countries. The 'old West' – the developed democracies of the United States and Europe – shows reasonably good economic health, coupled with an increasing preoccupation with improving the quality of life, which will one day also be attractive to the fast-growing countries. Mankind stands on the brink of its most hopeful century.

Yet you would hardly think so, listening to the political and economic debates in the United States and Britain today. Gloom prevails: the spectre of international terrorism stalks the streets (along with crime and CCTV). Climate change, we are told, will cause unprecedented natural disasters in a matter of years and threaten the very survival of the planet within decades. An economic slump is always around the corner. There is enough truth in all of these fears to make them plausible, and to make it essential for public officials to wrestle with them, as they do. Some 30 years ago the dangers were nuclear war, overpopulation and mass famine. Mankind, it seems, has a need for a sword of Damocles. It seems an irony of human nature that in times of adversity people come together and are cheerful and confront challenges, and in times of prosperity they grow apart, become self-obsessed and fearful.

In particular, there is a surreal, brittle and hysterical quality about international and security affairs today. The United States and Britain, at the official and press level at least (ordinary people usually being much more level-headed), seem to exist in a constant climate of fear and tension. The British government have proposed the longest period of suspension of the very pillar of British freedom, habeas corpus – the right of the individual not to be detained without charge – in modern history, even though the police and Department of Public Prosecutions have failed to come up with a single case in which this would have been necessary thus far. A grotesquely expensive identity card scheme which will encumber the ordinary citizen but surely be flouted by terrorists and criminals remains in development. Prevention of terrorism acts and new (and often unsought) police powers are rolled out in the Queen's Speech every year with monotonous regularity.

The United States has violated its own superb constitution by officially sanctioning torture (by calling it something else), the indefinite detention of 'terrorist' suspects without charge, kidnapping through 'extraordinary rendition', the use of secret military courts and the suspension of the Geneva Convention rules for the treatment of thousands of captured enemy combatants. The mantra constantly repeated by the US and British governments is that terrorism is the greatest foreign policy threat today – a 'long war', as great as the two world wars and Cold War of the last century.

A colossal Department of Homeland Security has been created with the admirable goal of protecting America from terrorist attack, but it also provides a giant bureaucratic mechanism of control using wiretapping without judicial authority and the Patriot Act (now thankfully being partially amended). It is an atmosphere reminiscent of the McCarthy 'witch-hunts' of the 1950s, except worse, because Senator Joe McCarthy influenced, but never controlled, the executive branch of government. Millions who travel by air in both countries will attest to the dreary reality of the bureaucratic mindset which authorizes officials to inflict the indignity of intrusive security checks upon millions of ordinary citizens, which can easily be avoided by those who are really determined.

We live in an artificially-induced climate of fear. Yet there is probably less to fear than at any time in our recent history. To paraphrase Franklin Roosevelt, 'there is nothing to fear but official fear-mongering'. Yes, the attacks of 9/11 were an atrocious act, as were the 7/7 bombings in London, and the attacks in Turkey, Madrid, Bali, Egypt, Morocco, Algeria and Pakistan attributed to al-Qaida and its affiliates. But terrorism is nothing new: ask the Northern Irish, Italians, Germans, Spanish, Indians, Sri Lankans, Algerians and Israelis, to name but a few. There have been no successful mainland attacks in the United States since 9/11, and only one post 7/7 in Britain, the amateurish affair of an improvized suicide attack on a regional airport, which killed or injured only the two alleged perpetrators.

The remarkable thing about Islamic terror is that, out of an Islamic population of several million in Europe – which some imaginative commentators have likened to a new Muslim invasion of the West – the actual number of attacks has been statistically insignificant. Public officials must never be complacent: there is every chance that a terrible atrocity is in the making and, doubtless diligent police work and intelligence have both played a major preventative role. But we should also remember the innate moderation of the overwhelming majority of Muslims, whose religion preaches a large measure of self-discipline in life, family and society, even if a few zealots indulge in interpreting its scriptures murderously, as Christians used to do hundreds of years ago (and some still do). A normally level-headed US former Centcom commander, General John Abizaid, recently claimed that Muslim fanatics number about 1% of the Islamic world, or 13 million, and the support group of fundamentalists behind them could number as many as 10%, or 130 million. Frightening figures indeed, until one realizes that they must be mere guesswork, round figures plucked out of a hat; 'close enough for government work', as the American military saying goes.

How does this compare, say, with the last century, in which the world was plunged into two global wars that took tens of millions of lives, while unprecedented machines of mass murder and tyranny were unleashed, taking up to 100 million lives and enslaving and terrorizing hundreds of millions more? This was followed by a Cold War in which millions also died in proxy wars across the globe, while mankind itself was faced by the possibility of massive reciprocal nuclear strikes that would have devastated the planet in minutes, as former presidential National Security advisers Henry Kissinger and Zbigniew Brzezinski make clear in their essays.

Even to pose the question is to recognize its absurdity. Of course there remain huge security challenges. Of course, if mismanaged, as they often are, these have the potential to become much worse: al-Qaida, it should be remembered, is a child of the West's attempt to harness Islamic extremism against the Soviet Union in Afghanistan. There is always a danger that in taking exaggerated action against a perceived threat the consequences reaped will be infinitely more dangerous than the original threat. Of course global warming is an enormous challenge, although surely not beyond man's technological means to master. The same is true of the problems of social inequality being caused by lopsided economic growth. But, uniquely, so far in this century the world does not face the spectacle of enormous military machines confronting each other and threatening to go to war. Two thirds of humanity now lives under more or less democratic regimes, while only one third did so just 30 years ago; the challenge is now to lift an equally large swathe of humanity out of misery, poverty and dead-end lives.

Iran is clearly an immediate challenge – as if the situation in Iraq were not serious enough, and indeed had not itself been a catalyst for Iranian ambitions, another example of the well-intentioned, ill-judged intervention going awry. With Iraq's collapse, and Iran's hugely expanded influence in southern Iraq and Baghdad, the large but rather decrepit state of Iran has made a huge leap forward towards dominating the Gulf without firing a shot. Iran is a much bigger player than Iraq ever was because it is much larger, with three times the population, and it dominates the entire north-eastern shoreline of the Gulf.

Iran, unlike Iraq, is unashamedly pursuing a 'peaceful' nuclear programme which will allow it to obtain weapon-grade uranium by around 2010, and possibly plutonium as well, and is continuing its long-range missile programme (even though it has probably suspended its development of actual nuclear warheads, as a somewhat misleading US intelligence assessment in late 2007 asserted). Iran is an unashamedly Islamic state, proselytizing Islamic revolution abroad and supporting terrorist movements. In short, Iran is a far more serious potential threat than Iraq ever was – which is why western governments supported Saddam Hussein as the lesser of two evils for so long. Iranian acquisition of nuclear weaponry conjures up the threat of nuclear blackmail and domination of the smaller Gulf states, as well as the somewhat remote chance of a nuclear exchange with Israel. Further, Iranian acquisition of the bomb would undoubtedly spark off a nuclear arms race in the region (as happened in Asia with the chain reaction of China–India–Pakistan), extending to Saudi Arabia, Kuwait, Egypt and possibly to Syria and Turkey as well.

For all of these reasons the present US administration must be supported in its resolve to prevent Iran from pursuing its nuclear programme without the safeguards that would make weaponization impossible: and that means that the option of military force should remain on the table – the current position of the Western allies. Those of us who vehemently opposed the invasion of Iraq are much more sober about the prospect of Iran's acquisition of nuclear weapons. Remember, few were opposed to the principle of the use of force to prevent Saddam's acquisition of nuclear weapons; they just wanted to see evidence that he actually *had* resumed a nuclear programme (in the event there was none). Iran makes no secret that it is pursuing a nuclear programme, making use of the loophole in the Non-Proliferation Treaty which permits this for peaceful purposes. However, Iran's past pursuit of a covert nuclear programme and weapons-related activities invalidates its credibility in asserting peaceful intentions. Quite simply, Iran cannot be allowed to reach the tipping point at which it can acquire nuclear weapons quickly.

It it would be absolutely wrong for any decision to use military force to be taken by an administration in the last months of office, and during a US election mired in the controversy over the US intervention in Iraq. Iran should undoubtedly be the first priority of the new administration that will be sworn in – in January 2009. All necessary means to prevent the country acquiring nuclear weapons must be used. There is time though: 2009, not 2008, is the year of Iran.

A diplomatic solution would be vastly preferred and, we believe, is obtainable. Such a resolution can be achieved if both sides tone down the rhetoric, establish a close mutual interdependence, and the West, while continuing to press Iran on its lamentable human rights record, accepts that 'regime change' is as unobtainable under pressure from outside as it was in the Soviet Union. Iran is a complex society, one with some elements of democracy and a nascent middle class, and should be fully engaged by the west economically, as Russia and China both were by the Nixon administration, in a 'grand bargain' in exchange for the renunciation of any nuclear ambitions that are anything other than verifiably peaceful, and an end to its support for terrorists abroad. An even worse legacy of the disastrous invasion of Iraq would be the adoption of a supine position towards Iran. Generosity and reaching out, but also firmness and clarity on the nuclear issue, should be the cornerstones of the West's Iran policy.

Another immediate challenge is the long-running and horrific genocide in Darfur, which has killed at least 200,000 people and displaced two million from their homes. The West should have intervened on humanitarian grounds at limited cost through imposing a 'no fly' zone and staging air attacks on the murderous but ragtag Janjaweed militia, surrogates for Sudan. At last a 36,000-strong UN force may be put into place – but is likely to be utterly ineffective without air support. Cynicism about Western motives is not dispelled when 'humanitarian' intervention takes place in, for example, oil-rich Iraq, but not in Rwanda or Darfur.

The Need for Change

Few can doubt that we are at a turning point in western international relations and security. There is a gale of change sweeping across the United States, blowing the country in a new direction after the experience of Iraq, which is as yet little more than a breeze in the foreign policy debate on the British side of the Atlantic. This is the theme of the American contributions to this short but crucial book from many of the UK's and the US's most senior and best-known policymakers from the most successful era of both countries' diplomacy.

Former US Secretary of State Henry Kissinger speaks of reality displacing the 'optimists and idealists', who believed in creating 'a full panoply of western democratic institutions' in the Middle East. Former Secretary of State George Shultz and Harry Rowen speak of a 'sense of drift and potential chaos'. Zbigniew Brzezinski, former Presidential National Security Adviser, speaks of having unintentionally united our enemies while dividing our friends. Former Presidential National Security Adviser General Brent Scowcroft suggests that the invasion of Iraq caused chaos in the Middle East. US Ambassador Charles Freeman paints a vivid and grim picture of the external challenges that the United States faces today: 'In Iraq the options are all bad and not improving'. Former US Defence Secretary Frank Carlucci says that 'despite our power, we cannot alone shape the world to our liking'. All of these urge the need for a more 'traditional' approach to US foreign policy, and for the reshaping of outdated post-Cold War international institutions.

Former President Jimmy Carter is unashamedly antagonistic towards the influence of US-style 'fundamentalists' on the outgoing Bush administration's foreign policy. Geoffrey Howe, former British Foreign Secretary and Deputy Prime Minister, speaks of the 'profoundly ill-judged' invasion of Iraq and its 'huge destructive consequences'. Former British Deputy Prime Minister and Defence Secretary Michael Heseltine admits to being 'deeply critical of the foreign policy of the present Bush administration'. Former British Energy Minister David Howell says America is 'no longer in charge'. British journalist Simon Jenkins speaks of 'the new middle ages'. The United Kingdom's foremost defence policy expert, Sir Michael Howard, bluntly labels the Iraq war 'a disaster' and 'a terrible error'.

It is wise to pay attention when men of this calibre concur. Unfortunately the foreign policy debate in the United Kingdom seems to be lagging well behind that in the United States, with neither the new Prime Minister, Gordon Brown, nor the Conservative opposition prepared even to admit to the enormous mistake made in Iraq, and the consequences thereof. We risk looking a little like the fanatical Japanese soldiers who went on fighting in the remote jungles of South East Asia long after the Pacific War had ended.

With only 15 months until the Bush administration leaves power, and with a new British government and reinvigorated Conservative party formulating new policies, now is clearly the time to contribute to the debate on US and British foreign policy. As the essays from our American cousins suggests, the United Kingdom still has much to contribute to the debate. Following a period of relatively benign neglect under the Clinton administration, the Bush administration's assertive interventionism abroad, while well intentioned, has clearly not worked. Rather than return to a period of introspection, the right way forward seems to be the kind of more realistic multilateral engagement advocated by Kissinger, Shultz, Brzezinski, Scowcroft, Nunn and Carlucci – albeit underpinned by the strong sense of US moral values urged by ex-President Carter. The senior Republican Foreign Relations Committee member Senator Richard Lugar also argues eloquently for the need not just for energy conservation in the West, but new multilateral western action to protect supplies of oil and natural gas.

* * *

On the British side, it seems fair to say that the Blair administration, in its ten years in office, embarked on the most radical foreign, defence and security policy in the United Kingdom's history, departing from the fundamental precepts that have underlain our approach to other countries for a couple of centuries or more. There is considerable agreement that a clean break should be made with the failed and already disastrous experiments in foreign policy of the last ten years. The British people demand nothing less. Merely 'finessing' the existing policy or making bureaucratic rearrangements such as creating a National Security Council (which will actually make things worse, further centralizing power in the hands of the Prime Minister, and a system which virtually broke down in the US during the Iraq war) will not work.

Traditional British foreign policy was constructed upon three unchanging pillars. The first was the defence and furtherance of British interests in the world. Particularly and most importantly, this was the protection of the British people themselves, and of the values that we pioneered of democracy, free speech, the rule of law and the individual rights of British citizens (in the current sterile debate about what constitutes 'Britishness', these about sum it up), as well as the furtherance of British economic interests in order to guarantee the continuing prosperity of the British people and their (now much reduced) dependencies.

Secondly, to secure these objectives, the United Kingdom has maintained a long tradition of the world's most effective fighting forces, at one stage being largely dependent on the navy, while more recently drawing on an effective army and air force as well. The United Kingdom has rejected the continental tradition of large conscripted armies, on the grounds that they are less efficient than professional armies, except in times of total war, and also for reasons of cost. In times of Empire our armed forces were expanded to defend our interests, paid for by the new wealth they brought in at the time. But over the past century our armed forces have been sparingly used, and only in defence of British interests which had been directly threatened, such as in the two world wars.

Thirdly, the underlying concern of British foreign and defence policy, which has endured several centuries, has been to preserve a balance of power in the world as it directly affects us. This has always made good sense. As long as the Continent across the Straits of Dover was not dominated by an overarching power, the United Kingdom could pursue its proper interests through diplomacy and alliances.

When a single power threatened to predominate – Spain in the sixteenth century, France in the eighteenth and early nineteenth centuries, Germany in the twentieth – British interests were considered threatened and we found ourselves in conflict until equilibrium was restored. With the Cold War and the coming of the superpower era, that seemed to have changed, but in reality it did not. The United Kingdom aligned itself with one of the superpowers, the United States, to resist the other, the Soviet Union, which appeared directly to threaten British interests and indeed the lives of all of our citizens. The end of the Cold War, however welcome, suddenly created an uncertain global landscape. It was in this unpredictable new world that the Blair government decided on its radical experiment in foreign policy. Different problems, it seemed, called for different solutions.

The Blair Experiment

What were the primary innovations of the Blair government? There was a new analysis of the dangers facing the United Kingdom, resulting in three responses that called for the demolition of the three traditional pillars of British foreign policy outlined above. The analysis was that, with the collapse of the Soviet Union, the United Kingdom no longer faced a direct conventional or nuclear military challenge. Thus the armed forces were at something of a loose end (the winding down of the United Kingdom's peacekeeping role in Ulster also contributed to this perception), and they could be freed up for a new mission. At the beginning of the twenty-first century, particularly after 9/11, the further view was taken that the world faced an insidious new challenge of 'asymmetrical' attack – small numbers of terrorists, mainly emanating from the troubled Middle East, capable of carrying war directly onto our own soil. Blair viewed this as even more pressing than that of Cold War mass annihilation through nuclear attack, and certainly one calling for a greater response in terms of placing the United Kingdom on a war footing with the consequent diminution of traditional civil liberties.

The three new responses born from this analysis were as follows. Firstly, as the British abandoned their primarily defensive posture, they had a proactive role to play (particularly in the early part of the Blair administration) in the enforcement of a new international order based on justice and help for the oppressed. Secondly, the United Kingdom should continue its Cold War close alignment with the United States even after this was no longer required to counterbalance the power of the Soviet Union. Indeed, this should be pursued more vigorously than ever, to the point of eclipsing virtually every other British interest. Thirdly, and most recently, the United Kingdom should espouse the Bush administration's policy of 'pre-emptive deterrence' – that is, striking at enemies perceived as potentially dangerous or hostile even before those enemies had actually done anything harmful to us. The backdrop to this was, of course, the 'war on terror', a war that the Bush administration claimed was as serious as World War I or II or the Cold War, and that was a 'long' war of indefinite duration at that.

Thus the United Kingdom was no longer acting to defend narrowly defined national interests – territorial, or in terms of protecting our people and their values – but in defence of vaguely drawn ideals of the greater good in places where our interests were not visibly involved at all. In order to achieve this it was proposed to risk the loss of British servicemen and women, and to spread our small but highly efficient armed forces more widely than ever across the globe. The United Kingdom abandoned its traditional balance-of-power diplomacy in favour of the role of enthusiastic subordinate to one great power on the argument, as I heard one senior foreign office official describe it, that 'the United States is so overwhelmingly powerful that we have to be on their side; it certainly wouldn't do any good to be seen to be against them' (although it is not even in the US's interests that we maintain this supine position).

This latter policy has been portrayed as simply a continuation of our old Cold War stance and traditional alliance with the United States, enshrined in NATO. But after the collapse of the Soviet Union, it is in fact a massive departure from the old policy. At no time in the United Kingdom's history have we identified our international security interests as being identical with those of a single great power – at least not since we were part of the Roman Empire or (arguably, because they were only a part of France) the Norman invasion. The United Kingdom's tradition of robust independence has thus been subsumed to that of an alliance with the strongest (but far from omnipotent) nation on earth, much as Austria–Hungary subordinated its foreign policy to that of Germany before World War I and Italy did to that of Germany in World War II (the subsequent fate of both countries is instructive).

Wars of Choice

How has the new Blairite foreign policy worked in practice? The idea of the United Kingdom acting as a kind of moral policeman or international conscience is, at first glance, quite attractive. If British forces do not face an international challenge of the kind they did during the Cold War or an internal one of the kind presented in Northern Ireland, then why not use them to pursue British moral values abroad, promoting democracy, human rights etc? These have been defined as 'wars of choice'. Blair's appetite for humanitarian wars – or, to their detractors, 'moral imperialism' – of this kind gradually increased over time, from intervention in Kosovo to Sierra Leone, to Afghanistan, to Iraq, to the current escalation in Afghanistan again.

There are a number of points to be made about such interventions. Firstly, it is not always predictable what the actual outcome of such interventions will be. Secondly, with the exception of Sierra Leone, four of the deployments have been American-led. Thirdly, even if the intervention does initially result in a favourable outcome, there is not always a clear exit for British forces without ending the benefits of such intervention and restoring the status quo or something much worse. In fact, our forces are still committed in all four countries.

Briefly examining each also explains why Blair became increasingly 'hooked' on these military adventures. The slide into benevolent intervention began in the last years of the Clinton administration, after two appalling humanitarian catastrophes appeared to underline that a hands-off approach to sectarian massacres was untenable. First there was the genocidal sectarian massacre of up to one million people in Rwanda, under the eyes of a small contingent of UN troops while the world averted its gaze. Then there was the prolonged period of inaction by the United States and its allies as Serbs massacred Bosnian Muslims until, finally, western governments were shamed into intervening – highly successfully, as a brief bombing campaign against Serbian positions soon brought them to the negotiating table and ended the war.

Thus encouraged, President Clinton and Prime Minister Blair embarked on their bombing campaign against Serbia to pre-empt a possible massacre of Kosovan separatists – which unfortunately occurred anyway. The issues were less clear-cut. Although the campaign ended successfully and also eventually toppled the Serbian strongman Slobodan

Milosevic, it was not entirely clear whether western intervention had precipitated the massacres or averted much worse ones. The endgame also proved protracted and messy. Still, on balance it could be judged a success and was clearly acceptable to western and, on the whole, global public opinion.

Blair then despatched British forces into Sierra Leone, to separate the combatants in a small but bloody civil war. The British forces performed their role superbly and this also ended well, although again the endgame has been protracted. When carried out for visibly humanitarian reasons to prevent massacres, it seemed that Blair's departure from using British troops solely in defence of our national interests (which actually belatedly began in Serbia under the Major government) was justifiable, even admirable, although there were some doubts about Kosovo.

Afghanistan

The real problem began with the US and British intervention in Afghanistan, which (like that in Kosovo) was under the auspices of NATO. This occurred in direct retaliation for the 9/11 attacks in the United States, carried out by extremists operating under the authority of Osama bin Laden and operating out of al-Qaida camps in Afghanistan. Shocking as the 9/11 attacks were, no direct British interest was at stake. Indeed the United States had for long done almost nothing to alleviate the UK's own terrorist problem in Northern Ireland – which resulted in more deaths altogether than 9/11 (and on a per capita basis four times as many) – but on the contrary permitted fund-raising and recruiting on its territory by the main terrorist organization, the IRA (the US was its principal source of funds outside the Irish Republic). It hardly bears imagining what the US reaction would have been to a major British bombing campaign on IRA bases across the border in the Irish Republic – a direct parallel with the US-backed invasion of Afghanistan.

It was asserted that the terrorist attacks of 9/11 were not so much an attack on the United States as upon the West as a whole, and therefore upon British interests. Yet not a single Islamic extremist attack had occurred in the United Kingdom up to then, and the UK has the vastly sensitive issue of a huge Muslim population, proportionately far exceeding that in the United States. Britons were killed in 9/11, but so indeed were many Muslims who just happened to be in the wrong buildings at the wrong time. There was a strong humanitarian case to be made for intervening against Afghanistan's obscurantist and repressive Taliban government, but not an overwhelming one. There were plenty of just as repressive regimes around the world.

The real purpose, as far as the United Kingdom was concerned, was to show solidarity and sympathy with the United States after 9/11. After a hesitant start the Taliban were dislodged, largely through a bombing campaign, from Kabul. It appeared that the intervention had been successful and, in the wave of sympathy after 9/11, acceptable to the British public. Doubts set in when the Americans seemed to want to leave the 'washing up' (the continued pacification of Afghanistan) for their allies. There was also the difficulty of establishing central authority under President Karzai, who has been described as the 'mayor of Kabul', against the traditional warlords of Afghanistan, the emergence of the country as the world's largest heroin producer, and finally with the return of a resurgent Taliban from the frontier provinces of Pakistan.

The United States and the United Kingdom had to decide whether to get out or continue to fulfil the role which they said they had come to perform, namely to defeat al-Qaida and keep the Taliban out of Afghanistan. The Blair government opted for the latter. This has involved increasing casualties among British forces, and has for now contained but not driven out the Taliban, which now occupies half the country again. Both Bush and Blair seem wholly oblivious to Afghanistan's history as a killing ground for local fighters, in rough terrain with which only they are familiar and which has repulsed virtually every previous foreign invasion. In the last century and a half this included the British three times and, most recently, the Russians, who failed to subdue the insurgents with an army of 150,000 men (around three times as large as the Allied force there today), sophisticated weaponry, tanks and aircraft as well as ruthless tactics. The current thinking that one more military push will save the country for democracy – ignores the Russian experience that the bigger the occupation force, the greater the resistance within Afghanistan.

While British participation in the initial NATO invasion could be defended on the grounds that keeping in with the United States after 9/11 was in the British national interest, its continuing presence cannot. What exactly are the British interests currently involved? What are our objectives? What has pacifying Afghanistan got to do with us? Surely we have more responsibility for resisting despotism in Zimbabwe, a British colony until 40 years ago, than in Afghanistan which we failed to subdue 150 years ago? True, drugs are a problem on British streets, but the western invasion has vastly boosted poppy production in Afghanistan (which in power the Taliban vigorously suppressed). Finally, is there any realistic prospect of subduing and controlling the country? The historical record and the escalating resistance today suggests not. Why did we go in, and why are we still there today in bigger numbers against a growing resistance? Is supporting and impressing the Americans a good enough reason?

Iraq

So to Iraq. This is not the place to rehash the arguments for and against the invasion in any detail, though Lord Howe ably and pithily alludes to them in his contribution. Suffice to say that one by one the pretexts for the invasion, as outlined by Blair to the House of Commons and the British people beforehand, and then modified subsequently, have fallen away. If Iraq had been producing and stockpiling weapons of mass destruction which threatened British forces (within 45 minutes of the decision to use them, according to Blair at the time), there would have been a pretext for invading. But Iraq had no such weapons, and the completion of the inspection by the UN team under Hans Blix the following autumn would have established that without the need to resort to war. If Iraq had been contemplating attack on its neighbours, there would have been a pretext. It was not.

If Iraq had had a hand in 9/11, a highly tenuous justification for British participation in the invasion might have been established. No such link has ever been shown, despite the best efforts of the Bush administration. Rather the reverse – Saddam Hussein regarded al-Qaida as a potential threat. If intervention had been useful to commercial and oil interests (not a very good reason for risking our servicemen's lives, but a British interest nonetheless), there might have been the ghost of a pretext. But Iraq's economy lies in ruins, oil production has actually fallen since the invasion, and American commercial interests have brusquely pushed the British aside from the lean pickings of the Iraqi carcass.

If the intervention had taken place for humanitarian reasons, to rid the world of an awful tyrant as Blair now repeatedly claims (although that was not the reason he gave at the time), there might have been a pretext. But as predicted by almost anyone with direct knowledge of the region the country has been plunged into a sectarian bloodbath, which by any estimate has already cost more lives in four years than under a quarter century of Saddam Hussein's rule and, in addition, has plunged the country into incredible hardship – with blackouts, shortages of water, food, medical supplies and petrol, massive violation of women's rights, and with nearly four million refugees internally and abroad.

The latest pretext, now advanced by former British Foreign Secretary Jack Straw, is that Iraq was already disintegrating and the West would have had to move in sooner or later. This of course directly and cynically contradicts the old line that Saddam was so strong as to constitute a serious military threat to neighbouring countries. While Saddam was probably too weak to embark on a new war, thanks to the no-fly zones and sanctions, there is not the slightest evidence of a relaxation of his repressive grip on the country, which would have led to disintegration. It is certainly on the verge of disintegration now.

Conservatives and Iraq

This brings us to an unnecessary dilemma for the opposition British Conservatives. The British people will not respect the Conservative party if it continues to justify or find semantic let-outs to excuse its support for the war in Iraq. The party should admit that it made an honest and understandable mistake. Like many well-meaning people, British Conservatives supported the invasion because they were told by the Prime Minister that there was a direct, imminent and very dangerous threat to British interests. The Prime Minister, of course, sits at the peak of our national security structure. Many backbenchers from his own Labour party were similarly assured. Although those who knew Iraq from direct experience were sceptical, it was entirely honourable for the Conservative party as a whole to rally behind the Prime Minister on an issue of grave national security, as oppositions have done many times in the past.

Now, however, Conservatives know that they were deceived. They know now that no such threat existed. It is no good Blair saying that he believed the threat existed then. He assured the country it existed, and produced evidence that was exaggerated, unsubstantiated or even outright false, to support him. Parliament and country were misled, and there is no shame in admitting that we were misled by a prime minister who hyped up the evidence and did not hesitate to invoke national security and patriotism to engage in a military attack that had no justification (in terms of either national security or British interests). To many, it was nothing less than our patriotic duty to rally behind the Prime Minister. We were told that, understandably, some of the intelligence for this could not be divulged. But when we realized we were misled, our indignation should have been all the greater.

Indeed it now seems that the invasion ran directly contrary to British interests. As much of British intelligence, many foreign affairs analysts and the British former minister Kenneth Clarke predicted at the time, it has turned a country that was formerly harshly controlled by Saddam, preventing terrorists operating overseas from his territory, into a breeding ground for extremists – with the United Kingdom as a prime target because of its role in Iraq – to the extent that home-grown extremists have taken up arms, as in the London terror attacks. (While these were utterly repugnant, it is not hard to see why unemployed Muslim youths in search of a cause might find one in the UK's role in the appalling carnage inside Iraq. The Blair government's attempt to claim that there was no connection between Islamic terrorism in the United Kingdom and the war in Iraq was puzzling. The connection is obvious to the overwhelming majority of the British people, as opinion polls have shown.)

That leaves, as the sole credible reason and justification for British actions in Iraq, Blair considering it in our national interest to 'fight alongside' the United States, in an action to which only a handful of allies, the biggest of which were Spain and Australia, also sent combat troops. This directly raises the issue cited at the beginning of this essay, namely our departure from balance-of-power politics to friend-of-the-strongest or subordination-of-power politics for the first time in centuries of our history. Is this in the UK's, or even the USA's, best interests?

The United Kingdom and the United States

The United States is easily the most powerful military and economic power on the globe. It has been a long-standing ally of the United Kingdom, based on the huge bond of a common language and many ties of kinship. Yet this should not obscure the fact that the United States is an independent and very different nation, being a continental power; one indeed which was forged in the fires of the War of Independence from the United Kingdom. As well as the US being the UK's closest friend, the UK is the US's oldest enemy. When the national interests of the two Atlantic powers have clashed, as they frequently have, the United States has not been sentimental in hesitating to oppose us.

The War of Independence was followed by the war of 1812 between the United Kingdom and the United States, the transatlantic naval clash over the slave trade and continuing rivalry in Latin America. The United States only joined very late in World War I (following German attacks on American shipping); argued with the United Kingdom at Versailles; then withdrew into isolationism, which was immensely damaging to a peaceful international order. Again, the United States joined World War II late, then initially tried to appease Stalin at Yalta. The old British quip that the Americans make the right decision 'in the end' is not without foundation.

After the war the United States was merciless in demanding its pound of financial flesh from the nearly bankrupt British economy, demanding payment in full for lend-lease and precipitating a run on the pound, and simultaneously pouring scorn on the 'socialist' post-war Labour government and British imperialism. The United States was ruthless in seeking to strip the United Kingdom of its colonial possessions, culminating in the withdrawal of financial support during the Suez crisis, which resulted in the failure of the expedition (however ill-advised it may have been in other respects). American commercial interests vigorously replaced British ones as the Empire declined, most notably in the oil-rich Middle East.

Up to now British governments have been reasonably clear-eyed about American intentions. Churchill, although half-American and romantically attracted to our ally, was well aware that our interests did not automatically converge, and spent much of the early war in effect attempting to seduce President Roosevelt to our side. In the post-war era Anthony Eden was effectively brought down by John Foster Dulles; Harold Macmillan skilfully constructed a father-son relationship with President Kennedy; and Harold Wilson manoeuvred to keep out of the Vietnam war while lending vocal support, much to the anger of President Johnson.

Margaret Thatcher, widely regarded in the United States as our greatest recent Prime Minister, always kept British interests at the forefront of her mind – not being afraid to challenge, often quite aggressively, her ideological soul-mate Ronald Reagan over the US's initially almost hostile position on the Falklands war, the US invasion of Grenada and the near abandonment of a common strategic nuclear stance at the Reykjavik summit. Fighting alongside the Americans during two world wars and the Cold War has created a huge empathy between the two nations. But this was also true of France, and relations have been much cooler. There are no such things as permanent friends in international relations, only permanent interests; the enemies of yesterday may be today's best friends, and vice-versa.

All of this seems obvious enough, and yet the Blair administration adopted a position of support for the foreign policies of whichever US administration was currently in power in Washington, regardless of the consequences. As already noted, it is hard to see what British interest is at stake in Afghanistan, much less Iraq, other than that of accepting the Bush administration's highly questionable premise that the world is engaged in an historic global war against terror. (In that context it is worth remembering that the total number outside Iraq and Afghanistan so far killed in this six-year-old 'war' is less than those who perished in a couple of hours fighting in D-Day, or a tenth of the number of civilians the UN says were killed in Iraq last year.)

Nor are there any obvious signs that the United Kingdom derives any advantage in terms of greater American respect. The Americans are a straight-talking people. One senior US diplomat recently told us that the US welcomes frank and honest disagreement from its friends: 'Perhaps that is what we lacked in the run-up to Iraq'. Another told us that 'Blair bears an immense responsibility for the war'. It has been asserted that Blair, far from seeking to slow Bush's rush to war, urged him to be tough, in an attempt to be 'more Catholic than the Pope'. The US Secretary of State, Condoleezza Rice, has indicated that the US is committed to dialogue with Europe as an entity, rather than to talking to individual countries. The United States does not want a divided European voice.

Rather than the weakened British government, German Chancellor Angela Merkel is the US's principal interlocutor in Europe now that the hated Gerhard Schroder is gone – and, like Mrs Thatcher, she is not afraid to criticize the United States (for example over Guantanamo) when necessary. Even France's new President Nicolas Sarkozy is now warmly welcomed in Washington. One may accept criticism from one's friends, because one knows they have one's interests at heart, whereas fawning and flattery can be just as harmful as outright enmity. Finally, however powerful it is, the United States does not control the world, as is painfully obvious from its misadventures in Iraq.

There might be something to be said for wholesale alignment with the United States if it had no challengers. But the United States, although powerful, is but the front runner in a world in which the European Union is just as big and rich, although less united and much less powerful militarily; Japan remains a huge economic and military force; Russia remains a huge continental and nuclear military power; and China, India and Brazil are all emerging as regional giants. It simply doesn't make sense for the United Kingdom to be seen, as it is by so many across the world, as the US's poodle.

Of course there is a very serious common security problem, in particular that of global terrorism and the growing ability of terrorists to cross borders. There is also to some extent a related problem of nuclear proliferation, which is perhaps the single biggest security challenge in the early part of the twenty-first century. It must be the United Kingdom's primary foreign policy priority to limit the spread of nuclear weapons. But there are other huge challenges as well – those of the competing nationalisms between China, Japan and Russia for example, or between China and India; the global environmental challenge; economic globalization itself; the security of oil supplies; the fight for scarce water resources; global poverty. This is not to mention the appalling mess at the heart of the oil-rich Middle East as a result of the war in Iraq, and the long-standing sore of Israel–Palestine. These problems are not soluble by blind allegiance to the United States, and a new administration in the US may shift its emphasis away from the war on terror to these wider issues. Indeed the United States shows signs of facing up to the massive failure of its policy in Iraq sooner than the United Kingdom does. A new US administration with a new policy will not thank the United Kingdom for its cheerleader role in the conflict.

In addressing these huge new problems, it is surely better for the United Kingdom to return to its traditional three principles – defence of British national interests, conservation of the men and women in its armed forces so that they can be used where they are really needed, and balance-of-power diplomacy – rather than to stick to Blair's new policies which have already entangled us in two probably unwinnable wars and cost dozens of service lives. Meeting an anxious father whose son was serving in Iraq, one of us was asked should the young man be killed, what would he actually have died for?

We muttered the usual platitudes, but the honest response would have been 'blowed if I know'.

The United Kingdom's posturing has also been at the expense of areas of traditional interests. Thus the UK's armed forces have been damagingly overstretched, as Lord Heseltine argues here. It also seems incredible that the Russian security services can appear to reach out and eliminate a British citizen in London without the kind of immediate mass expulsion of Russian spies (most of their embassy staff) that used to occur in the past. Many months later just four were expelled. It is astonishing that Iranian-made bombs can be used to target British vehicles in Basra without a huge and public Foreign Office outcry; or that Zimbabwe's dictator Robert Mugabe, who inherited control of a British crown colony, can terrorize and starve his people with no more than a slap on the wrist from Labour ministers; or that a genuinely horrific humanitarian disaster can occur in Darfur with little international action being advocated by the British government; or that our former Prime Minister could cite 'national security' as a reason to halt a judicial investigation into allegations of corruption in the awarding of British contracts in Saudi Arabia; or that the United Kingdom can run down so many of its embassies in energy rich central Asia, as Sir John Coles points out, or in Latin America, just as that continent has entered a new era of largely stable democracy and economic growth. While our army fights boldly alongside the Americans, the Foreign Office seems to have its hands tied in protecting our own interests.

One theme that recurs throughout the following essays, for example those of Lord Howe and Sir John Coles, is the Blair government's arrogant, wanton and almost complete disregard for the traditional institutions of British government and parliament in formulating foreign policy. Hordes of partisan 'special advisers', consisting of people with often very little experience, have bypassed the Foreign Office, expert ambassadors, military chiefs and the intelligence services to pursue objectives and policies of their own. The government has shown little interest in impartial advice from sources with real knowledge and experience in its blind pursuit of its own goals and of 'spinning' stories to its advantage.

The historical backdrop of the government's mistakes is magisterially and eloquently set out by Professor Sir Michael Howard. The issue of how best to utilize our superbly professional but compact armed forces is addressed in the contributions by Lord Heseltine, former Defence Secretary, while the limits on the Foreign Office itself are eloquently set out by the former Permanent Secretary, Sir John Coles, and Sir Mark Allen – who also urges a more gradualist and sensitive approach to promoting democracy in the Middle East. Simon Scott Plummer and Branko Terzic draw attention to the enormous environmental challenges facing the planet, to which Senator Lugar also refers. And I have tried to suggest some of the changes in the institutional framework for intervention that might be considered.

A paradox facing foreign policymakers, as set out in this book, is to return to more traditional, limited and realistic foreign and security policy goals while still engaging in, not shying away from, the huge common challenges of an interdependent world. The multiple security challenges are complex and potentially very dangerous. But to end on an optimistic note, the prize is of handing on to our children a world in which prosperity is much greater and more widely spread than ever before, in a secure international environment.

1

RECLAIMING THE VALUES OF
THE UNITED STATES

Jimmy Carter

Americans have always been justifiably proud of our country, beginning with our forefathers' bold Declaration of Independence and their pronouncement that 'all men are created equal, that they are endowed by their Creator with certain inalienable rights, that among these are Life, Liberty and the pursuit of Happiness'. Since then our people have utilized the US's great natural resources, access to warm oceans, relatively friendly neighbours, a heterogeneous population and a pioneering spirit to form a 'more perfect union'.

Now, more than at any time in history, the United States of America has become the pre-eminent military power on earth. While there has been a sharp downward trend in worldwide expenditures for weapons during the past 20 years, the United States has continued to increase its military budget every year. It now exceeds $400 billion annually, equal to the total of all other nations combined. The next largest military budget is Russia's, which is one-sixth as large. The only arms race that we are having is with ourselves. One reason for this enormous expenditure is that 20,000 sailors and marines are deployed in ships afloat and almost 300,000 additional troops are stationed in more than 120 countries, with military bases in 63 of them. Since I left office in 1981, American presidents have intervened about 50 times in foreign countries. In addition to supplying our own military forces, the US's arms manufacturers and those of our NATO allies provide 80% of weapons sales on the international market.

Our people have been justifiably proud to see the US's power and influence used to preserve peace for ourselves and others, to promote economic and social justice, to raise high the banner of freedom and human rights, to protect the quality of our environment, to alleviate human suffering, to enhance the rule of law and to co-operate with other peoples to reach these common goals.

With the most diverse and innovative population on earth, we have learned the value of providing our citizens with accurate information, treating dissenting voices and beliefs with respect, and accommodating free and open debate on controversial issues. Most of our political leaders have extolled state and local autonomy, attempted to control deficit spending, avoided foreign adventurism, minimized long-term peacekeeping commitments, preserved the separation of church and state, and protected civil liberties and personal privacy.

All of these historic commitments are now being challenged.

What has aroused these sharp disputes and, at the same time, engendered such profound departures from the US's traditional values? One factor is our nation's reaction to the terrorist attack of September 11, 2001, as we realized the intensity, permanence and global nature of terrorism. Another change is that massive sums of money are being injected into the political process, with the exercise of unprecedented influence by special interests within the increasingly secretive deliberations of government.

The Disturbing Trend to Fundamentalism

The most important factor is that fundamentalists have become increasingly influential in both religion and government, and have managed to change the nuances and subtleties of historic debate into black-and-white rigidities and the personal derogation of those who dare to disagree. At the same time these religious and political conservatives have melded their efforts, bridging the formerly respected separation of church and state. This has empowered a group of influential 'neo-conservatives', who have been able to implement their long-frustrated philosophy in both domestic and foreign policy. The influence of these various trends poses a threat to many of our nation's historic customs and moral commitments, both in government and in houses of worship.

Our nation has declared independence from the restraints of international organizations and has disavowed many long-standing global agreements, including judicial decisions, nuclear arms accords, controls on biological weapons, environmental protection, the international system of justice and the humane treatment of prisoners. Even with our troops involved in combat and the United States facing the threat of additional terrorist attacks, we have neglected alliances with most of the very nations we need to have join us in the long-term fight against global terrorism. All these political actions have been orchestrated by those who believe that the utilization of our nation's tremendous power and influence should not be constrained by foreigners. Regardless of the costs, some leaders are openly striving to create a dominant American empire throughout the world.

Based on these premises, it is no longer considered necessary to observe restraints on attacking other nations militarily, provided often uncertain intelligence sources claim that their military or political policies might eventually be dangerous to the United States. When branded an 'axis of evil' they are pariahs, no longer acceptable as negotiating partners, and the lives of their people tend to become relatively inconsequential.

There has been a disturbing trend toward fundamentalism in recent years, among political leaders and within major religious groups both abroad and in our country, and they have become increasingly intertwined. I felt the impact of this movement for the first time when Ayatollah Khomeini assumed the leadership of Iran, branded the United States of America 'the Great Satan', and encouraged his young and militant followers to hold 52 of our embassy personnel captive for 14 months. This shameful action was a direct violation of international law. His fundamentalist interpretations of the Islamic Holy Scriptures, on which he based his religious leadership, also contravened the traditional teachings of the Koran concerning peace, compassion and, specifically, the benevolent treatment of visitors or diplomats from other nations.

For generations, leaders within my own church and denomination had described themselves as 'fundamentalists', claiming that they were clinging to the fundamental elements of our Baptist beliefs and resisting the pressures and influence of the modern world. This inclination to 'cling to unchanging principles' is an understandable and benign aspect of religion, and a general attitude that I have shared during most of my life.

I soon learned, however, that there was a more intense form of fundamentalism, with some prevailing characteristics:

1. Almost invariably, fundamentalist movements are led by authoritarian males who consider themselves to be superior to others and, within religious groups, have an overwhelming commitment to subjugate women and to dominate their fellow believers.

2. Although fundamentalists usually believe that the past is better than the present, they retain certain self-beneficial aspects of both their historic religious beliefs and of the modern world.

3. Fundamentalists draw clear distinctions between themselves, as true believers, and others, convinced that they are right and that anyone who contradicts them is ignorant and possibly evil.
4. Fundamentalists are militant in fighting against any challenge to their beliefs. They are often angry, and sometimes resort to verbal or even physical abuse against those who interfere with the implementation of their agenda.
5. Fundamentalists tend to make their self-definition increasingly narrow and restricted, to isolate themselves, to demagogue emotional issues, and to view change, cooperation, negotiation and other efforts to resolve differences as signs of weakness.

To summarize, there are three words that characterize this brand of fundamentalism – rigidity, domination and exclusion.

One of the most bizarre admixtures of religion and government is the strong influence of some Christian fundamentalists on US policy in the Middle East. Almost everyone in the United States has heard of the *Left Behind* series by Tim La Haye and Jerry B. Jenkins, 12 books that have set all-time records in sales. Their religious premise is based on a careful selection of Bible verses, mostly from the Book of Revelation, and describes the scenario for the end of the world. When the Messiah returns true believers will be lifted into heaven, where, with God, they will observe the torture of most other human beings who are left behind. This transcendent event will be instantaneous, and the timing unpredictable. There are literally millions of my fellow Baptists and others who believe every word of this vision, based on self-exaltation of the chosen few along with the condemnation and abandonment, during a period of 'tribulation', of family members, friends and neighbours who have not been chosen for salvation.

It is the injection of these beliefs into the US's governmental policies that is a cause for concern. These believers are convinced that they have a personal responsibility to hasten this coming of the 'rapture' in order to fulfil Biblical prophecy. Their agenda calls for a war in the Middle East against Islam (Iraq?) and the taking of the entire Holy Land by Jews (occupation of the West Bank?), with the total expulsion of all Christians and other gentiles. This is to be followed by infidels (Antichrists) conquering the area, and a final triumph of the Messiah. At this time of rapture, all Jews will either be converted to Christianity or be burned.

Based on these premises some top Christian leaders have been at the forefront of promoting the Iraqi war, and make frequent trips to Israel to support it with funding and lobby in Washington for the colonization of Palestinian territory. Strong pressure from the religious right has been a major factor in the US's quiescent acceptance of the massive building of Israeli settlements and connecting highways on Palestinian territory in the West Bank. Some Israeli leaders have utilized this assistance, while conveniently ignoring the predicted final plight of all Jews.

This has helped to bring about another dramatic departure from the American opposition to settlement activity that prevailed during the previous four decades, beginning when Dwight Eisenhower was president and extending through the terms of his successors until 1993, when President Bill Clinton gave almost blanket approval to settlement expansion. President George H. Bush had been especially forceful in opposing specific Israeli settlements between Jerusalem and Bethlehem, even threatening to cut off financial assistance to Israel.

Although some encroachment on Palestinian territory can be accommodated in future peace negotiations, current Israeli plans to retain far-reaching West Bank settlements and to expand a large enclave known as Ma'aleh Adumim from deep within the West Bank all the way into East Jerusalem will likely spell the death knell for prospects for the 'road map for peace', the keystone of President George W. Bush's Middle

East policy. This will be a tragedy for the Israelis and the Palestinians.

The Threat to US Civil Rights

This triumph of civil rights at home did not preclude the US's acceptance and support of some of the most brutal foreign regimes in our hemisphere and other regions, which blatantly violated the human rights of their own citizens. As a newly elected president, I announced that the protection of these rights would be the foundation of our country's foreign policy, and I persistently took action to implement this commitment. It has been gratifying to observe a wave of democratization sweep across our hemisphere and in other regions, as the fundamental rights of freedom were respected.

During the past four years there have been dramatic changes in our nation's policies toward protecting these rights. Many of our citizens have accepted these unprecedented policies because of the fear of terrorist attacks, but the damage to our reputation has been extensive. Formerly admired almost universally as the pre-eminent champion of human rights, the United States now has become one of the foremost targets of respected international organizations concerned about these basic principles of democratic life. Some of our actions are similar to those of the abusive regimes that we have historically condemned.

Following the attack of 9/11, the US government overreacted by detaining more than 1,200 innocent men throughout the United States, none of whom were ever convicted of any crime related to terrorism. Their identities have been kept secret, and they were never given the right to hear charges against themselves or to have legal counsel. Almost all of them were Arabs or Muslims, and many have been forced to leave the US.

To legalize such abuses of civil liberties, the Patriot Act was hurriedly enacted. Leading opponents of some of its provisions are very conservative and well-known Republicans who have organized groups known as Patriots to Restore Checks and Balances, and Free Congress Research and Education Foundation. The President has called for the law to be expanded and made permanent, but even the conservative 'patriots' have deplored such provisions as authorization for federal agents to search people's homes and businesses secretly; to confiscate property without any deadline or without giving notice that the intrusion has taken place; and to collect without notice personal information on American citizens, including their medical histories, books checked out of libraries and goods they purchase. The government can now seize an entire database – all the medical records of a hospital or all the files of an immigration group – when it is investigating a single person. Although most of the disputed sections of the Patriot Act are not focused on sus- pected terrorists but apply to the general public, government leaders have succeeded in having them extended or made permanent.

A large number of men and some young boys have been captured in the wars in Afghanistan and Iraq and transferred to an American prison camp in Guantanamo, Cuba, where about 520 people from 40 nations have been incarcerated and held incommunicado for years, almost all without legal coun- sel and with no charges levelled against them. It has also been confirmed by US officials that many have been physically abused.

After visiting six of the 25 or so US prisons in Iraq, the International Committee of the Red Cross reported registering 107 detainees under 18, some as young as eight years old. The journalist Seymour Hersh reported in May 2005 that Defense Secretary Donald Rumsfeld had received a report that there were '800-900 Pakistani boys 13–15 years of age in custody'. The International Red Cross, Amnesty International and the Pentagon have gathered substantial testimony of the torture of children, confirmed by soldiers who witnessed or participated in the abuse. In addition to personal testimony from children about physical and mental mistreatment, a report from Brigadier-General Janis Karpinski, formerly in charge of Abu Ghraib, described a visit to an 11-year-old detainee in the cell block that housed high-risk prisoners. The general recalled that the child was weeping, and 'he told me he was almost twelve', and that 'he really wanted to see his mother, could he please call his mother'. Children like this 11-year-old have been denied the right to see their parents, a lawyer or anyone else, and were not told why they were detained. A Pentagon spokesman told Mr Hersh that 'age is not a determining factor in detention'.

Physicians for Human Rights reported in April 2005 that 'at least since 2002, the United States has been engaged in systematic psychological torture' of Guantanamo detainees, that has 'led to devastating health consequences for the individuals subjected to it'. The prisoners' outlook on life was not improved when the Secretary of Defense declared that most of them would not be released even if they were some day tried and found to be innocent.

The terrible pictures from Abu Ghraib prison in Iraq have brought discredit on our country. This is especially disturbing since US intelligence officers estimated to the Red Cross that 70 to 90% of the detainees at this prison were held by mistake. Military officials reported that at least 108 prisoners have died in American custody in Iraq, Afghanistan and other secret locations since just 2002, with homicide acknowledged as the cause of death in at least 28 cases. The fact that only one of these was in Abu Ghraib prison indicates the widespread pattern of prisoner abuse, certainly not limited to the actions or decisions of just a few rogue enlisted persons.

The participants at a recent Carter Center conference on human rights were in broad agreement that recent policies of the United States were being adopted and distorted by opportunistic regimes to serve their own interests. They told of a general retreat by their governments from previous human rights commitments, and emphasized that there was a danger of setting back democratic movements by decades in some of their countries. Participants explained that oppressive leaders had been emboldened to persecute and silence outspoken citizens under the guise of fighting terrorism, and that this excuse was deflecting pressure coming from the United States and other powers regarding human rights violations. The consequence was that many lawyers, professors, doctors and journalists had been labelled terrorists, often for merely criticizing a particular policy or for carrying out their daily work. We heard about many cases involving human rights attorneys being charged with abetting terrorists, simply for defending accused persons.

Equally disturbing were reports that the United States government is in some cases contributing directly to an erosion of human rights protection, by encouraging governments to adopt regressive counter-terrorism policies that lead to the undermining of democratic principles and the rule of law, often going far beyond the US Patriot Act.

At the conference we all were encouraged because the most onerous of the new US policies were being questioned in the Congress and through the federal court system, and would ultimately be corrected. Although many legal issues had not yet reached the final appellate level to be clarified, most contested domestic cases had been resolved favourably, and the United States Supreme Court ruled in June 2004 that US federal courts 'have jurisdiction to consider challenges to the legality of the detentions of foreign nationals captured abroad in connection with hostilities and incarcerated at Guantanamo Bay'.

In most of the countries represented at our human rights conferences – including young democracies – such checks and balances in the judicial system are not so well developed, and make the questioning and reversal of abusive policies much less likely.

Another subject of concern was that the early use of military force and an announced policy of pre-emptive war sent a signal that violence had become a much more acceptable alternative to peaceful negotiations in the resolution of differences. The general consensus of these experts on democracy and freedom was that policies based on violence always result in a cycle of escalated violence.

Still Very Much a Nuclear World

When American leaders gave the official announcement to Russia in 2001 that we would pull out of the ABM Treaty (Anti-Ballistic Missile Treaty), it was predictable that Russia would respond by announcing plans to upgrade its nuclear forces without regard to existing arms control treaties.

The end of the US's 'no first use' nuclear weapons policy has aroused a somewhat predictable response in other nations. Chinese Major-General Zhu Chenghu announced in July 2005 that China's government was under internal pressure to change its 'no first use' policy: 'If the Americans draw their missiles and position-guided ammunition onto the target zone on China's territory, I think we will have to respond with nuclear weapons'.

Until recently all American presidents since Dwight Eisenhower have striven to restrict and reduce nuclear arsenals – some more than others. So far as I know, there are no present efforts by any of the nuclear powers to accomplish these crucial objectives. The world is crying out for positive leadership from Washington, and there are some important steps that could be taken.

It should be remembered that the enormous nuclear arsenals of the United States and Russia still exist. Little bilateral effort has been made to reduce these unnecessary weapons, with mandatory verification of such agreements and the dismantling and disposal of decommissioned weapons. With massive arsenals still on hair-trigger alert, a global holocaust is just as possible now, through mistakes or misjudgements, as it was during the depths of the Cold War.

The Russians retain vast stockpiles of nuclear weapons, and refined materials for the building of others. Rogue states or terrorists would take any steps to obtain these loosely guarded and valuable products. In 1991 US senators Sam Nunn and Richard Lugar sponsored legislation that helped finance commitments by the United States and Russia to join in the proper disposal of these stockpiles, but this wise and effective program is in danger because of a recent lack of adequate financing and the inability of the two governments to agree on access to Russian sites and liability if anything goes wrong.

There is also an important opportunity for progress within NATO, which needs to de-emphasize the role of its nuclear weapons and consider an end to their deployment in Western Europe. Despite its dramatic eastward expansion, NATO is retaining the same stockpiles and policies it had when the Iron Curtain divided the continent and many of its new members were potential targets for our nuclear missiles.

Another historic international commitment that is being abandoned is limitation on the further testing of existing nuclear weapons and the development of new ones. In August 1957 President Eisenhower announced a proposal to ban the further testing of nuclear explosives, and faltering progress has been made since that time. While I was president, there were strict global limits on the testing of any explosive above 150 kilotons, which at that time was the smallest that could be monitored. Subsequently it became technologically feasible to detect very small explosions, and a Comprehensive Nuclear Test Ban Treaty was evolved. It has been signed and ratified by Russia, France and the United Kingdom, and signed but not ratified by China and the United States. Although President Bill Clinton signed the treaty and pledged that it would not be violated, the most recent American budget refers, for the first time, to a list of possible US tests that would violate the treaty.

Another radical shift in policy that causes concern even among our closest allies is the US's move toward deployment of destructive weapons in space. The ABM Treaty prohibited space-based weapons, but our government's abandonment of the treaty in 2002 opened the door to this extremely destabilizing project. The new Defence Department doctrine defines our goal as 'freedom to attack as well as freedom from attack' in space. The goal is to strike any target on earth within 45 minutes. As described by the US Air Force one method, named 'Rods from God', would hurl cylinders of heavy metals to strike a target at 7,200 miles per hour, with the destructive force of a small nuclear weapon. Although no official presidential directive has been revealed, the Pentagon has already spent billions of dollars developing such weapons and planning for their deployment. The government announced plans in June 2005 to begin production of plutonium-238, a highly radioactive material that is used almost exclusively as a power source for space vehicles. There is little doubt that a global treaty to ban space weapons will leave the United States safer than a unilateral decision to put the first (and certainly not the only) weapons in space.

Even within our government, sharp disagreements have been revealed about what should be done with some of the key components of our ageing nuclear inventory. Among approximately 5,000 active warheads known to be in our nation's arsenal, the key weapon now deployed on submarines is called the W76, about which I was thoroughly briefed as President. It was designed during the Cold War to be as small and powerful as possible, within a thin and fragile case. The current argument is whether to refurbish the ageing warheads or replace them with a new model. In addressing this issue, there will be great pressure to renounce completely the global ban on nuclear testing, precipitating a new arms race as other nations would almost certainly take the same action.

Nuclear proliferation is an increasing source of instability in the Middle East and in Asia. Iran has repeatedly hidden its intentions to enrich uranium while claiming that its nuclear program is for peaceful purposes only. This explanation has been given before, by India, Pakistan and North Korea, and has led to weapons programs in all three nations. As Iran moves down the same path, direct diplomatic effort by the United States with an 'axis of evil' nation is inconceivable. American leaders must rely on European intermediaries and threats of military action, with implications of support if Israel were to strike at Iran's nuclear facilities. At the same time, Israel's uncontrolled and unmonitored weapons status entices leaders in neighbouring Iran, Syria, Egypt and other Arab nations to join the nuclear weapon community.

The fact is that the global threat of proliferation exists, and the destructive actions of several non-nuclear nations – and perhaps even some terrorist groups – will depend on lack of leadership among those who already have powerful arsenals but are not willing to restrain themselves. Like it or not, the United States is at the forefront in making this great moral decision. Instead of setting an example for others, we seem to be choosing proliferation.

Iraq and Terrorism

A basic question to be asked is this: 'Has the Iraqi war reduced the threat of terrorism?' Unfortunately, the answer is no. Not only have we lost the almost unanimous sympathy and support that was offered to us throughout the world after the attack of 9/11, but there is direct evidence that the Iraqi war has actually increased the terrorist threat. In testimony before the Congress, CIA Director Porter Goss stated, 'Islamic extremists are exploiting the Iraqi conflict to recruit new anti-US jihadists [holy warriors] … These jihadists who survive will leave Iraq experienced and focus on acts of urban terrorism'. He added that the war 'has become a cause for extremists'.

To corroborate his opinion, the US National Counter-Terrorism Centre reported that the number of serious international terrorist incidents more than tripled in 2004. 'Significant' attacks grew to more than 650, up from the previous record of about 175 in 2003. Terrorist incidents in Iraq also dramatically increased, from 22 attacks to 198, or nine times the previous year's total – after the US handover of political authority to an interim Iraqi government. It is obvious that the war has turned Iraq into the world's most effective terrorist training camp, perhaps more dangerous than Afghanistan under the Taliban. Also, instead of our being able to use Iraq as a permanent base from which to pressure Iran and Syria, there seems to be a growing allegiance between the evolving Iraqi government and its fundamentalist Shiite neighbours, which may greatly strengthen Iran's strategic position in the Middle East.

The adoption of pre-emptive war as an American policy has forced the United States to renounce existing treaties and alliances as unnecessary constraints on our superpower's freedom to act unilaterally. Another serious consequence of this policy is the likelihood that other aggressive nations will adopt the same policy of attacking to remove leaders they consider to be undesirable.

* * *

It is good to know that our nation's defences against a conventional attack are impregnable, and it is imperative that the United States remain vigilant against threats from terrorists. But as is the case with a human being, admirable characteristics of a nation are not defined by size and prowess. What are some of the other attributes of a superpower? Once again, they might very well mirror those of a person. These would include a demonstrable commitment to truth, justice, peace, freedom, humility, human rights, generosity and the upholding of other moral values.

There is no inherent reason that our nation cannot be the international example of these virtues. In achieving these goals, our great country should strive in every practical way to co-operate with other nations, most of which share the same fundamental ideals. There is an unprecedented opportunity as we enter this new millennium to use our unequalled influence wisely and with a generous spirit.

There would be no real sacrifice in exemplifying these traits. Instead, our own well-being would be enhanced by restoring the trust, admiration and friendship that our nation formerly enjoyed among other peoples. At the same time, all Americans could be united at home in a common commitment to revive and nourish the religious faith and historic political and moral values that we have espoused and for which we have struggled during the past 230 years.

2

THE POST-WESTPHALIAN WORLD

Henry A. Kissinger

I have been a policymaker and a professor. I have therefore experienced the different perspectives from which to view international affairs. As a professor I could choose my subjects, and I could work on them for as long as I chose. As a policymaker I was always pressed for time, and I had to make decisions in a finite time frame. As a professor I was responsible primarily for coming up with the best answer I could divine. As a policymaker I was also responsible for the worst that could happen. As a professor the risk was that the important would drive out the urgent. As a policymaker the risk was that the urgent would drive out the important. So how to find the right perspective?

The role of the church, as Pope John Paul II said to me once, is to stand for truth, and truth cannot be modified according to the contingencies of the moment. I agreed with that as a philosophical statement. The prophet deals with eternal verities. The policymaker lives in the world of the contingent; he or she must deal with partial answers that hopefully are on the road to truth. Contingent answers are always somewhat inadequate, but the attempt to achieve the ultimate in a finite period of time can produce extraordinary disasters. Crusades have caused even more casualties than wars of national interest. Therefore, how to balance the road to the ultimate with the needs of the moment is what policymakers have to deal with.

The unique aspect of the current international situation is that, for the first time in history, it is global in a genuine sense. Until the end of World War II the various continents pursued their histories almost in isolation from each other. There was no significant way, except by trade, that the Roman Empire and the Chinese Empire could interact with each other. The same was true through the centuries that followed with respect to the various empires and institutions in different parts of the world.

For 200 years Europe was the dominant element in international affairs. What we consider international relations today really dates back only to the Treaty of Westphalia of 1648. After the suffering caused by religious wars, a new international concept was needed. That international concept had various elements, introducing for the first time the notion of sovereignty – that countries were supreme within their borders and that no other country had the right to intervene in their domestic affairs. The borders defined the reach of international law. The use of force across borders could be defined as illegal or as aggression.

Then, in the eighteenth century, the sovereign state became identified with the nation. It was a new idea that legitimacy was established by grouping people of a common language in the same political institution. As a result, the international politics that developed were based on a multiplicity of sovereign states. Peace depended on two attributes. Firstly, a certain equilibrium of power was required, meaning that no nation should be strong enough to dominate the others. Secondly, the notion of justice of the various states had to be sufficiently comparable, so that they did not solve all their problems by force. These attributes of the European system were later defined as 'international relations'. China never lived in a world of equal states. It was always the most powerful state in its region until it became a subject of foreigners in the nineteenth century. China never had to live in a system of equilibrium with its neighbours and, until the twentieth century, no Asian state participated until Japan emerged.

The international system is now global. It is also instantaneous. In the nineteenth century, it took three weeks for a message to get from London to Vienna. Therefore, at the Congress of Vienna it was not possible to instruct the Ambassador by telling him what to say. He had to be instructed in the concepts of foreign policies. This had the enormous advantage that it obliged the ministries to outline their strategic concepts. Today ambassadors or plenipotentiaries are instructed precisely on what to say, which means that at home people think primarily of the next day or the next week, and they are not obliged by the diplomatic process to conceptualize their foreign policies.

Of course, it had never happened that one could observe what was occurring in real time. All of this accelerates policy-making to a point that makes it extraordinarily difficult to develop the concepts that are needed at the moment when concepts become more and more important. The international system is in a state of upheaval, but there are different kinds of upheaval in different parts of the world. One characteristic is that the nation and the state, as we have known it, are in the process of transformation in most parts of the world. Some of what were thought of as universal principles of international relations are therefore changing.

In Europe the nation-state is in the process of being diminished. The European Union is supposed to replace it, but the reality is that Europe is in transition between a past that it has rejected and the future which it has not yet reached. Until the middle of the twentieth century the European nation-state could appeal to its citizens for great sacrifices on behalf of the nation. Today the European nation-state can demand much fewer sacrifices. To be willing to sacrifice one has to believe in the future as being more important than the present. When the satisfaction of the present becomes a principal aim, the capacity for sacrifice for either domestic or international politics diminishes.

Therein resides one of the deeper causes of disagreement between Europe and the United States. The United States is still a nation in the traditional sense and, rightly or wrongly, it can demand sacrifices of its people. For most Europeans now, peace is an overriding objective, and that affects the capacity to conduct traditional foreign policy. For all these reasons, for the North Atlantic countries the so-called 'soft' power issues become the dominant issues in their relation to each other and to other nations.

Globalization Becomes a Dominant Issue

In this manner globalization has become a dominant issue. A gap is opening up between the economic world and the political world. The economic world runs on globalization, but the peoples of the world live in nations. The impact of globalization is inherently differential; it is in the nature of the market. Those who suffer setbacks as a result expect help from their governments, and governments seek to bring about reform. But there is no real structure for the necessary sacrifices. As a result, governments can lose respect even when the economy is growing. Polls in almost every country show that there is less confidence in governments than there was previously. That may be due to the quality of the government, but it may also be inherent in the situation.

The globalized world faces two contradictory trends. The globalized market opens prospects of heretofore unimagined wealth. But it also creates new vulnerabilities to political turmoil and the danger of a new gap, not so much between rich and poor as between those in each society that are part of the globalized, internet world and those who are not. The impact of these new trends on the developing world is profound. In economies driven by a near imperative for the big to acquire the small, companies of developing countries are increasingly being absorbed by American and European multinationals. While this solves the problem of access to capital, it brings about growing vulnerabilities to domestic political tensions, especially in times of crisis.

The Asian states, by comparison, are still nations in the original sense, with quite well-recognized international borders which conduct foreign policy on the basis of a strategic assessment that they make of the role they can play in the world, on the impact they can have on their neighbours and on the consequences they want to bring about by their conduct. The states are larger than the European model. In China many provinces have a larger population than the largest European countries. Japan is the second largest economy in the world. Each of these countries is undergoing a transition of its own. Japan at this moment is moving from a period when acquiescence of the American leadership role was the condition of its economic growth, and when Japan did not conduct a very active foreign policy, into considering three options – one, to continue the present relationship with the United States; two, to adopt an independent course in elaboration of the national interest; three, to move towards Asia, and even towards China, into some sort of community. At this moment Japan is still committed to the American relationship, but the discussions beneath the surface are looking at these options in a way that has not happened previously.

Then we have the situation in Korea, which is fundamentally an issue of whether it is possible to bring about the denuclearization of North Korea. The US, China, Japan, Russia and South Korea all agree that North Korea should denuclearize, yet have so far proved unable to impose their will on a country of 20 million with the most decrepit economy in the world and the most oppressive government. Every step of the way is contentious. The fact remains that if denuclearization is not achieved, the impact on the rest of the world in demonstrating how one becomes a nuclear power is so enormous that it simply cannot be permitted.

China

If anyone had told me during my secret trip to China in 1971 what the Chinese economy would look like today, I would have thought it was a fantasy. In 1971 China had no consumer industry and no automobiles, no significant heavy industry, no trade with the United States. When we opened to China, one of the moves we made to show the Chinese that we were willing to deal with them was to permit American tourists visiting Hong Kong to buy $100 worth of Chinese-manufactured goods. Now China is running a huge export surplus. Recently I made a speech in China in which I said that the rise of China is inevitable. And that is true. We must get used to that proposition. There is nothing we can do to prevent China from continuing to grow. Nevertheless, I received some letters after my speech asking if I was implying that the United States is on the decline. My answer is that, no, I am not saying the United States is on the decline, but the outcome of the rise of China depends importantly on how we handle international affairs from here on in.

But first China has enormous problems of its own to tackle. At any moment there are 100 million Chinese on the road, looking for jobs, coming from the countryside into the cities. The cities require a new infrastructure. The interior of China is at the level of the least developed countries. The coast of China is at the level of the most advanced countries. It has never before happened that a country could develop in this manner. That is the big challenge to the Chinese. This is why for the next decade or so, they will not engage in international adventures.

At the same time the influence of the Chinese, because of their economic capacity, their political skill and their growing military strength in the surrounding countries, is going to grow. It is a twofold challenge for western strategy – one, to remain engaged in Asia; two, to see whether the next generation of Chinese can develop a sense that the United States and the western world are potential partners rather than permanent adversaries. That will determine how China will use its strengths in 10 or 15 years from now. It is also the fundamental challenge that we face in that relationship.

It is partly a cultural problem. American history dates back 200 years, which is shorter than the history of most individual Chinese dynasties. Americans are convinced that they have the best governmental system in the world. But the Chinese managed 4,000 years of history before the United States ever existed, and therefore they react neuralgicly to American lectures on how they should reform themselves. Americans are very pragmatic. They think every problem has a solution, and that that solution can be achieved in a very brief period of time. By contrast the Chinese think in a more historical, long-term manner. So one of our big tasks in the decades ahead is how to mesh the long-range thinking of the Chinese with the practical thinking of the United States.

The Middle East

In the long term the challenge of Asia may be the most important. In the short term the challenge of the Middle East is the most dangerous. The Middle East is in the position of Europe in the seventeenth century before the Treaty of Westphalia. It has no firm foundation because almost all the states were created after World War I by foreign countries to suit their own interests. The nation has even less meaning because its borders do not coincide with ethnic realities and so, therefore, the Middle East is organically in turmoil. When a religious ideology of a fundamentalist nature is added to that mix, dialogue collapses because dialogue must be based on the premise that there is some objective criterion, like reason, while fundamentalism recognizes only one truth.

The religious wars of the seventeenth century were ended by exhaustion. The challenge of our times is whether these can be ended by reason before a catastrophe or by exhaustion afterwards. But reason requires a western presence and incentives to bring about some kind of equilibrium.

Two issues confound the international community on the Middle East above all others – Palestine and Iraq. The argument that the Palestinian issue is the key to Middle East peace is only partially valid. The issue of radical Islam transcends the Palestinian issue. It is important, therefore, that an outcome on Palestine be clearly achieved by moderate leaders rather than radical pressure. In some respects the conditions for this are favourable. There is consensus about the outcome (even in Israel). The 1967 borders would remain, except for the settlements around Jerusalem; Palestine would be a demilitarized state with its capital in the Arab part of Jerusalem; refugees would return only to the Palestinian state. What is lacking are governments in both Israel and among the Palestinians that are strong enough to bring it about. The United States, the European Union and moderate Arab states need to co-operate to develop a plan and then conduct the negotiations to implement it.

The challenge of Iraq is far more complex. Optimists and idealists posited at the beginning that a full panoply of western democratic institutions can be created in a timeframe that the American political process will sustain. Reality is likely to disappoint these expectations. Iraq is a society riven by centuries of religious and ethnic conflicts; it has little or no experience with representative institutions. The challenge is to define political objectives that, even when falling short of the maximum goal, nevertheless represent significant progress and enlist support across the various ethnic groups.

Western democracy developed in homogeneous societies. Minorities found majority rule acceptable because they had a prospect of becoming majorities, and majorities were restrained in the exercise of their power by their temporary status and by judicially enforced minority guarantees. Such an equation does not operate where minority status is permanently established by religious affiliation and compounded by ethnic differences and decades of brutal dictatorship. Majority rule in such circumstances is perceived as an alternative version of the oppression of the weak by the powerful. In multi-ethnic societies, minority rights must be protected by structural and constitutional safeguards. Federalism mitigates the scope for potential arbitrariness of the numerical majority, and defines autonomy on a specific range of issues.

Four political objectives for Iraq should be:

1. To prevent any group from using the political process to establish the kind of dominance previously enjoyed by the Sunnis.
2. To prevent any areas from slipping into Taliban conditions as havens and recruitment centres for terrorists.
3. To keep Shiite government from turning into a theocracy, Iranian or indigenous.
4. To leave scope for regional autonomy within the Iraqi democratic process.

However it was started, whatever was done unwisely, what is our immediate problem? The outcome in Iraq will shape the next decade for American foreign policy. A debacle would usher in a series of convulsions in the region as radicals and fundamentalists move for dominance, with the wind seemingly at their backs. Wherever there are significant Muslim populations, radical elements would be emboldened. As the rest of the world related to this reality, its sense of direction would be impaired by the demonstration of American confusion in Iraq. A precipitate American withdrawal would be almost certain to cause a civil war that would dwarf Yugoslavia's, and it would be compounded as neighbours escalated their current involvement into full-scale intervention.

A total collapse of a western presence may make negotiations impossible. The challenge is to maintain an equilibrium sufficient to convince all the parties to negotiate a standstill. There have to be three levels. Firstly, there has to be a negotiation between the various parties in Iraq. Secondly, there should be a negotiation between the neighbours of Iraq and the permanent members of the Security Council and Egypt, as a major interested party, about the international status of what comes there. And thirdly, there should be a negotiation including all of these countries, plus countries with a large Muslim population (like Indonesia, India and Pakistan) and countries that have a big interest (like Japan and Germany) that are not permanent members of the Security Council, to embed a stabilized Middle East into an international system.

The lesson everybody needs to learn is that nobody can achieve all their objectives. Anyone who tries to achieve all of their objectives will produce a chaotic situation, in which they won't be able to achieve even their minimum objective.

The Anti-Globalization Backlash

Many thoughtful observers rely on economic growth and the new information technology to move the world more or less automatically into the new era of global well-being and political stability. But this is an illusion. World order requires consensus, which presupposes that the differences between the advantaged and those disadvantaged who are in a position to undermine stability and progress be of such a nature that the disadvantaged can still see some prospect of raising themselves by their own effort. In the absence of such a consciousness, turbulence, both within and among societies, will mount.

The world's leaders – especially in the industrialized democracies – cannot ignore the fact that in many respects the gap between the beneficiaries of globalization and the rest of the world is growing, again both within and among societies.

Globalization has become synonymous with growth; growth requires capital; and capital seeks the highest possible return with the lowest risk, gravitating to where there is the best trade-off between risk and return. In practice this means that, in one form or another, the United States and the other advanced industrialized countries will absorb an overwhelming percentage of the world's available investment capital.

Multinational companies based in the United States or Europe emerge increasingly as the engines driving globalization. For them the rush to size has turned into a goal in itself, almost compulsively pursued, because the ability to drive up the stock prices of their company is becoming the standard by which chief executives are increasingly judged. As executives turn from being long-range builders into financial operators driven by shareholder value determined in daily stock market quotations, the vulnerability of the entire system grows, its long-term vitality could be weakened and, even more so, its resilience in times of crisis. And within the developing countries it creates political temptations for attacks on the entire system of globalization.

In the process the typical developing country's economy bifurcates. One set of enterprises is integrated into the global economy, mostly owned by international corporations; the rest, cut off from globalization, employs much of the labour force at the lowest wages and with the bleakest social prospects. The 'national' sector is substantially dependent on its ability to manipulate the political process of the developing country. Both kinds of companies pose a political challenge – the multinationals because they seem to withdraw key decisions affecting the public welfare from domestic political control the local companies because they generate political pressures on behalf of protectionism and in opposition to further globalization.

The social world reflects this two-tiered system. Globalized elites – often living in fortified suburbs – are linked by shared values and technologies, while the populations at large in the cities are tempted by nationalism, ethnicity and a variety of movements to free themselves from what they perceive to be the hegemony of globalization, frequently identified with American domination. The global internet elite is completely at ease with the operation of a technologically-based economy, while a majority, especially outside the United States, Western Europe and Japan, neither shares this experience nor may be prepared to accept its consequences, particularly during periods of economic hardship.

In such an environment attacks on globalization could evolve into a new ideological radicalism, particularly in countries where the governing elite is small and the gap between rich and poor is vast and growing. A permanent worldwide underclass is in danger of emerging, especially in developing countries, which will make it increasingly difficult to build the political consensus on which domestic stability, international peace and globalization itself depend.

Iran Graver than Iraq

Let me turn finally to a totally new level of international structure. For the first time there are now universal issues that cannot be dealt with on a regional basis and to which the balance of power is no answer. One that my personal fate has obliged me to deal with is the issue of nuclear proliferation. If I were to define what issue concerned me most when I was in government, it was the issue of what I would do if the President ever said he had no other recourse except nuclear weapons. The reason it preoccupied me is because, in the nature of the job, I knew better than most people what the consequences would be. On one level I thought nobody has a moral right to make a decision involving the death of tens of millions. On another level I knew that if this was proclaimed as our attitude, we would turn the world over to the people who have no hesitation in committing genocide. I never had to resolve that issue because there was only one other nuclear country, the Soviet Union, which, however much it was a rival, calculated the costs of nuclear war in a comparable way.

Now, if you have 15 nuclear countries and every leader has to make his or her own calculations, and if these countries do not have the intelligence systems and the technological ability to protect their weapons, then we will live in a world in which some catastrophe becomes nearly inevitable. It is an accident of history that Iran has become the test case, after which it is impossible to conceive that nuclear proliferation can be stopped. This issue is graver than the situation in Iraq. Its solution has one aspect that the West can undertake by itself. Two leading Republicans and two leading Democrats who have held high office in the United States – George Shultz, myself, Senator Sam Nunn and former Democratic Secretary of Defence William Perry – recently co-authored an article in which we said that the nuclear countries need to make visible sacrifices in their nuclear weapons if they want to ask other countries to give up nuclear weapons. I would say this is an overriding issue.

Looking at the energy world, when demand rises faster than supply, it is inevitable that conflicts must develop if it is attempted to be dealt with on a non-general basis. On environment, countries like China and India are, in a way, right if they point out that we had a head start in which the world was polluted yet now we are trying to stop them. But on the other hand it does not change the fundamental issue.

The German philosopher, Emmanuel Kant, wrote an essay in the eighteenth century in which he said some day there will be universal peace. The only issue is whether it will come about by human insight or by catastrophes of such a magnitude that we have no choice. His words were right then and they are right today, although some of us may add that it may take some divine guidance and not just insight to solve the problem.

3

PROTECTING THE GOLDEN MOMENT

George P. Shultz and Harry Rowen

A truly outstanding feature of the world today is the strength
of the economy on a global scale. Expansion is taking place in
most countries and all regions of the world. A world once split
by the Cold War now operates as a global economy, able to
raise standards of living by a broader application of the law of
comparative advantage. Low-income-per-capita countries, as
in the case of China, India, Brazil, now Indonesia and others,
are experiencing rapid economic advances. New middle
classes are emerging. Poverty, while still a huge problem, is
going down. Of course, there are problems. Some people's
incomes are rising faster than others, as is always true, but relatively few people are worse off absolutely than before. In
many respects, you could say the world has never been at such
a propitious moment. In this respect, a golden age is upon us.

At the same time there is more tension than ever in the
world as weapons of mass destruction appear in more hands,
the international system for limiting their spread erodes and
loosely structured arrays of Islamic extremists (some supported by Iran) use the weapon of terror. The nation-state, the
historic way of organizing civilized life and governmental

activity, is under attack, and all too many parts of the world are not governed effectively. Such places, used by terrorists for training and launching attacks, are a grave danger to the civilized world.

The diplomatic task for the future, then, might be called 'protecting the golden moment' from assaults by radicals who want to change the system and who use violence indiscriminately – the weapon of terror – as a primary means of persuasion. How is this task to be accomplished?

First of all we should be careful not to undermine the conditions that have helped make the world economy flourish. Today in the United States, and also more widely, there is a growing sentiment that would put sand in the gears of trade with the aim of trying to protect specific jobs. If this sentiment is translated into legislation, much damage will be done – including harm to European and American workers. We and other countries have been there before, notably between the two world wars, and should know better than to return to those grim times. This means being careful about booby traps. For instance, you can be strong supporters of improving the environment on a global, let alone national scale, while being skeptical about imposing environmental requirements on openness to trade. Protectionism painted green is still protectionism.

A second objective in the economic area is to encourage further development. Many Muslims, especially Arabs, see themselves – correctly – as having missed out on the last several centuries of industrial development. Arguably, a necessary condition for their politics to change for the better is for them to catch up economically. For perspective, it is useful to remember that not very long ago both China and India were widely seen as mired in poverty and stuck there with hopeless politics. Among Islamic countries the Arab states have been especially held back by the appeal of destructive socialism and authoritarianism and, for some of them, by the well-known 'oil curse'. The latter are now flush with money, but the record shows that this situation might not endure. They need better economic policies, and they now have more examples to look at than just the already wealthy countries. This implies moving away from policies that are often ostensibly populist but that actually protect their elites. So they need to produce goods and services (other than oil-related ones), and the ways to do this are now on display around the world.

We can help ourselves by using less oil and thereby reducing our vulnerability. At the same time a lower oil price would induce producers to turn to more useful work. Economic development based on human effort, not just the exploitation of oil wealth, can lead to more open political systems. We must encourage that kind of development in Islamic lands and communities. But for this to work there must be a demand for their products (other than oil), so sustained world growth and open trading arrangements are needed for them to grow.

Looking at the problem from a diplomatic perspective we have to recognize that today's world is more fractured than in recent times. A sense of potential chaos is combined with a dependence on oil that has a long history. That dependence is now resulting in huge uncertainties, because the areas where the oil is located are in many cases highly unstable. The uncertainty is also propelling vigorous work in scientific, venture capital and other areas in a search for ways to use oil more efficiently as well as to find alternatives.

In addition, the sense of drift and potential chaos is fed by the inability of established institutions to function effectively. The UN Security Council, even when a strong statement is issued, typically fails to follow through with tough action. This, of course, is usually because the members in fact don't agree and this, in turn, leads to a search for other – non-Security Council – ways to deal with urgent, indeed potentially life-threatening, matters.

The structure for dealing with current issues is loose and elusive. The Cold War was a period of serious tension, with a palpable danger of massive nuclear destruction, so we said good riddance to it. However, its structure was easy to understand, with two superpowers, some additional important countries, and many smaller ones. They tended to be aligned with one side or the other. Even the non-aligned movement was, in many ways, subject to the disciplines of the Cold War stand-off. In a sense, you could say that it was a period when there were relatively few known variables and two big and clear constants. The current period is different in that the simplicity and discipline of the Cold War have eroded drastically. Now we see a world with more variables and with constants that are not as strong, becoming semi-variables themselves. The result is that the world is harder to understand and therefore more uneasy, even though the tension of the Cold War has been relieved.

Diplomacy, Strength, Gradualism and Realism

So all this means that we in the United States, and in other countries as well, face a radically changed world with rising powers, ungoverned territories, radical Islamists and immensely powerful weapons spreading around. This situation requires a much larger and invigorated commitment to the tasks of diplomacy, conducted on a global scale. We in the United States could be worse off. Colin Powell, in his time as Secretary, saved the Department of State from a downward slide. He reinvigorated the recruitment process, improved the resource base and technological capability, and raised the spirits of the foreign service. But much more needs to be done. The size of the foreign service needs to match global needs, the means need to be developed to retain access to the services of senior people and more political appointees of high quality need to be brought on board.

What ideas can underlie the diplomatic effort? Here are several that have proven useful in earlier times:

1. Change toward freedom and openness is possible, but requires patience.

2. Political openness usually proceeds in tandem with economic development, not ahead of it.
3. Strength of purpose and capability are essential.
4. Strength and diplomacy are intertwined and are mutually reinforcing.
5. A deep and continuing consultative process among like-minded people is needed to create understanding necessary to make hard choices.
6. A successful strategy must be based on realism and sustainability.

When considering our work on any problem, we should ask if these ideas are being applied and, if not, why not? To paraphrase Teddy Roosevelt, even if you have a big stick, speak softly, firmly, and in a manner that will be sustained by the evolution of facts. Remember that tricks can be played by asymmetric warfare, and look out for surprises.

A guiding idea in the struggle against terrorism is the notion of prevention. If we can help prevent the spread of hateful ideology, then we have taken the first essential step. There are antidotes to terrorism in all Islamic societies, not least because terrorists are killing large numbers of Muslims. Indonesia, Malaysia and the Philippines – countries with large numbers of Muslims – show that governments can strengthen these antibodies by mobilizing public support against the terrorists and by avoiding indiscriminate suppression of dissent. Outsiders can help, but only in a low-key way.

Remember too that the strategy of prevention is consistent with the idea that change is possible if prevention can be sustained. Look at Algeria today where, as reported by the *New York Times*, 60% of the enrolment in colleges is by women. They are filling an increasing array of jobs, making up 70% of Algeria's lawyers and 60% of its judges. This is hardly consistent with stereotypes of what is possible in a predominantly Muslim society.

Strength is always a key – not only economic and ideological strength, but also military capability, willpower and the self-confidence to act when necessary. A special challenge is created by the potentially devastating consequences of a terrorist attack. Huge numbers of lives are lost, in addition to destruction of property and economic damage and dislocation. The need for sharply improved intelligence capability is obvious. Knowledge about attacks before they take place is essential. We then have an uncomfortable decision to make, especially when the culprit group or individuals are in a country where terrorists are tolerated or even assisted. But the decision is always difficult. Intelligence is hardly ever clear-cut, targets can be elusive and may be embedded in civilian surroundings, and consequences may be hard to predict. Intelligence is widely discredited now because of its failures in 9/11 and Iraq. Nevertheless, the failure to use preventive force in such circumstances can have consequences that are simply not acceptable. And the consequences are not limited to the immediate damage. The precedent of inability to act carries implications for the future.

Two Challenges: Global Warming and the Nuclear Threat

Perhaps we can also gain some momentum for this agenda of strength, co-operation, prevention and diplomacy from the pursuit of two big ideas on a global scale. Each one is drawn from the Ronald Reagan playbook.

First, can we find our way to a global structure that allows us to attack the issues of global warming? The Kyoto Protocol could not work because the concept behind it has no chance of global acceptance. No one should expect that countries such as China or India can accept an agreement that amounts to a cap on their economic growth. The Montreal Protocol, which we developed during the Reagan period, was an international agreement to phase out the production of materials that were depleting the ozone layer of the atmosphere. When the agreement was completed, Ronald Reagan called it a 'magnificent achievement'. Work remains to be done on this problem. Nevertheless, the Protocol has been implemented with such wide support that former UN Secretary-General Kofi Annan called it 'perhaps the most successful international agreement to date'. It worked in part because every state knew it would feel the problem and so took part in the solution. The effort was and is action oriented. The only feasible way to move ahead with global warming is to act piecemeal, to do what can be done now. And remember, one size does not fit all. In this respect, Montreal has a lot to teach post-Kyoto. We can put ideas that work into play once again.

Second, can we find our way to a world free of nuclear weapons? We are both working on this problem on a non-partisan basis with Sam Nunn, William Perry, Henry Kissinger, Sid Drell and Max Kampelman, along with many others. We take a cue from development of that idea at the 1986 Reykjavik meeting between President Reagan and General-Secretary Gorbachev. Many steps need to be taken, and with great care. Each one presents difficulties and requires hard work and, in some cases, skilful diplomacy. Success would almost surely have desirable after-effects.

The use of nuclear weapons has never made sense. Now, as they spread, the likelihood that they will be used rather than merely relied upon for their deterrent value grows, with potentially disastrous consequences. The steps essential for progress to a world free of nuclear weapons are desirable in and of themselves. In some cases the steps interact with other objectives, as in the effort to deal with global warming. More use of nuclear power seems likely and desirable, since electricity is produced without greenhouse gases.

But that cannot go forward comfortably under present circumstances. A basic fact of technology complicates the ability to limit access to nuclear weapons. Readily fissionable material usable in bombs is present in either the fuel going into nuclear power stations or in the spent fuel. This implies that the possessor of such power stations is technically within a short distance of being able to make explosives. The prospect for building more nuclear power plants implies the wider distribution of potential bomb material. So the goal of international control of the nuclear fuel cycle takes on added urgency. This would be a return to a version of the earlier Acheson-Lilienthal Plan, in which nuclear power would have been controlled by an international agency. That plan foundered on the rock of the Cold War, leaving us today with a weak and crumbling bulwark against widespread access to bomb materials.

We face another nuclear hazard – an unnecessary one. Long after the end of the Cold War hundreds of missiles in the United States and Russia are on alert, ready to be launched in minutes, possibly at each other. Although equipped with electronic safeguards, having them in this condition in such numbers is an invitation to disaster and should be ended. The goal of a world free of nuclear weapons, and success in taking the steps necessary to achieve that goal, calls for a vigorous diplomatic effort on a multinational scale. The dangers growing in the Middle East suggest a concentrated focus on that region. Although the difficulties of achieving it would be great, the alternative to a nuclear-weapon-free zone in the Middle East is fearsome to contemplate.

The pursuit of big ideas on a world scale might well generate just the sense of cohesion that would help like-minded nations face down other problems that threaten our peace and our prosperity. At the same time, a little Cold War history reminds us that unpleasant realities can change if we confront them with strength, cohesion and sustained diplomatic effort.

4

BRITISH FOREIGN POLICY:
THE FOLLY OF IRAQ

Geoffrey Howe

The need to recreate British foreign policy springs from the serious damage done to most of its components, as a consequence of the profoundly ill-judged Anglo-American invasion of Iraq and subsequent response to the onslaught on Lebanon. Just three days after the savage tragedy of what we have come to know as 9/11, I spelled out in the House of Lords the four conditions which would, in my then view, need to be fulfilled if the United States was to be justified in taking any military action against any target:

1. Such action would have to be justified on the basis of deterrent self-defence and not, in any way, as retaliation or 'response'.
2. There would need to be robust evidence ('as sure as one can be', I said) of the responsibility for the 9/11 brutality of the party so to be attacked.
3. Maintenance of the long-term unity of international support would be essential to success. (Without that robust evidence, I stressed, this third condition would not be fulfilled.)

4: Any such action 'must be accompanied by a renewed commitment to tackle even-handedly both sides of the Middle East conflict. The USA, as the principal guarantor of Israel's very existence – and not only the United States – needs to be seen as equally committed to support for the legitimate rights and expectations of the Palestinian people'. (In today's circumstances this is perhaps the most important proposition.)

It is now as clear as crystal that, in relation to the Iraq war, not one of those four conditions has ever, or yet, been fulfilled. And along with many others I have to acknowledge my own responsibility for having failed, in the months and years which followed, to focus upon and underline that comprehensive absence of justification for going to war.

What has been the result? I leave aside the hugely destructive consequences in and for Iraq itself. On the wider scene the misguided and mistaken 'war on terrorism', with predictably provoked counter-attacks, has spread and escalated across the world. The mutual confidence of NATO partners in each other was seriously damaged, as was also, though to a lesser extent, the capacity of EU member states to formulate and apply a concerted and constructive foreign policy of the kind required. Worse almost than all that, the worldwide stock of sympathy and goodwill towards the United States has largely disappeared – along with the earlier, long-standing respect for the wisdom of British policy towards the problems of the Middle East – which had once prevailed almost throughout that region. And all this in a world where tense foreign policy threats and crises are more than likely to arise or persist, from Teheran to Taiwan, from Tbilisi to Pyongyang and who knows where else?

Several propositions are almost bound to apply to the management and resolution of such problems. In the first place, they all need to be tackled and, if possible, resolved by means of diplomacy and not by force. As David Cameron said in his thoughtful speech a few months ago: 'There are more tools of statecraft than military power'. That diplomacy will almost always need to be multilateral. And, with a little less certainty, the United States is more than likely to be required to play a major part.

The United Kingdom's Role

What role for our own country? In contrast to the age when I was active on the foreign field, the great majority of purely 'British problems' (mainly post-imperial) have largely passed away, or at least diminished in importance. I mean no disrespect when I mention, for example, Hong Kong, Gibraltar and even Northern Ireland. Certainly it is hard today to identify any problem for which British foreign policy, on its own, can be expected to provide the answer. Our response would almost always need to be in partnership with one or more other countries. Our history, reputation and experience would still often offer a diverse choice of partners – the most often forgotten, perhaps, being those within the Commonwealth, whose value we all too often discount. But more often than that, we are likely to find ourselves sharing interests with our partners and neighbours in the European Union. Acting alone, not one of us is likely to be able to make an effective input into global diplomacy. Europe divided is all too likely, as Iraq has plainly demonstrated, to emerge as Europe disregarded – Europe without influence.

This is far from being a novel thought. In July 1984, more than 20 years ago, as Margaret Thatcher's Foreign Secretary and with her full authority, I circulated a document entitled *Europe: The Future*:

> The Ten [then EC member states] have the weight and must show more political will to *act* together: concentrate their efforts where their leverage is greatest and their interests most directly touched e.g. in the Middle

East and Africa; and recognize that influence does not last if not backed by the necessary resources ... *The objective should be the progressive attainment of a common external policy.*

If that was true in 1984, then it is of even greater importance at the present time.

Nowhere is the effective application of a common European policy more necessary today than in relation to the Middle East. That too was recognized by the leaders of the European Community as long ago as 1980. Once more I draw attention to the policy then promoted by the United Kingdom (when Peter Carrington was Margaret Thatcher's Foreign Secretary) and endorsed by EC colleagues in the Venice Declaration (13 June 1980). Again I quote:

The time has come to promote the ... implementation of the two principles universally accepted by the international community: the right to existence and to security of all the states in the region, including Israel, and justice for all the peoples, which implies the recognition of the legitimate rights of the Palestinian people [including the right] to exercise fully its right to self-determination.

But would not a robust European stance on this issue risk damaging the long-standing transatlantic partnership, whose continuance remains of fundamental importance to world peace? Emphatically not. It would be in the interests of the United States as much as of the rest of the world for Europe (embracing, of course, the United Kingdom) to be making a more positive contribution to global peace and security. The transatlantic partnership, if it is to be restored and maintained, certainly does need to be rebalanced – *both* ways, with Americans taking more account of the need for legitimacy, for partnership, for mobilizing world opinion and for working within the United Nations.

Europeans need to do far more to pull their weight together and on the global stage, not just in the formulation of effective foreign policy but also in enhanced defence co-operation. In no way would that be intended to be, or have the effect of, pitting Europe against the United States in some kind of challenge. On the contrary, the framework for that kind of partnership in the Middle East already exists. As the International Crisis Group Declaration reminded us on 4 October 2006, it is, of course, the 'roadmap' proposed in 2003 by the Quartet (UN, US, EU and Russia). I quote from the ICG document, of which I was one of 135 signatories: 'If the Arab-Israeli conflict, with all its terrible consequences, is ever to be resolved, there is a desperate need for fresh thinking and *the injection of political will'*. For our country to put its full weight behind this multilateral approach would be to amplify, and certainly not to subordinate, the impact of British foreign policy upon the world in which we live.

Foreign Policy Failures

What are the immediate lessons of the foreign policy failures of the Government? The relationship in particular between the Prime Minister and each of the three Secretaries of State (who hold what used to be called the great offices of state – the Foreign Office, the Exchequer and the Home Office) is of enormous importance. In this context there is the need for continuous close collaboration between No. 10 Downing Street and the Foreign and Commonwealth Office. Some people will recall the rather mischievous comment of Sir Nicholas Henderson, when he said that he had noted the customary ill-humour of the Foreign Secretary when accompanying the Prime Minister on visits abroad – which is nevertheless nothing to compare to their mood if there is any suggestion of their being left behind. That indicates the nature of the relationship that should exist.

In modern times that relationship is much more difficult to maintain, because each of the two characters concerned can fly around the world several times a week scarcely seeing each other from one day to the next. Moreover, there was a tendency, certainly under the Blair administration, for the appointment of personal envoys to double or overlap the work of the Foreign and Commonwealth Office. One final feature is the extent to which the Prime Minister, if alone on missions of great importance, can receive adulation and adoration that can impair his or her judgement. It is worth recalling that Mr Blair was in Washington within a few days of 9/11 and attended the joint session of both Houses of Congress. Even without making a speech, he received two standing ovations. That kind of thing can seriously impair the judgement of a British Prime Minister.

Certainly, as others have pointed out, it is clear that from the outset of this dismal story that wholly insufficient attention was paid to the wisdom, experience and expertise available in our diplomatic service. Likewise, the intelligence services were treated with less respect than they ought to have been. To make matters worse, since then the resources available to the Foreign and Commonwealth Office have been almost continuously reduced. At the same time that the People's Republic of China is opening embassies and Confucius Institutes around the world (and not least throughout Latin America and Africa), we are closing the equivalent places. It is crucial that that kind of attitude towards the specialist agencies, whose services we need to take advantage of, should no longer be sustained or repeated.

Nothing more clearly indicates the need for cabinet government than the 2004 report of the privy councillors under the chairmanship of Lord Butler on Iraq war intelligence. It clearly highlighted the resources of wisdom, experience and expertise available in the independent civil service, not least in the Foreign and Commonwealth Office and not to mention Cabinet ministers themselves, which was almost systematically neglected throughout that period. The privy councillors expressed 'concern about the informal nature of much of the government's decision-making process'; the so-called 'sofa government'. They drew attention to the fact that 'excellent quality papers were written by officials, [but] these were not discussed in cabinet or cabinet committee', and expressed the view that that process 'risks reducing the scope for informed collective political judgment. Such risks are particularly significant' in the field of foreign affairs. All this is a consequence of the casual, ill-considered, thought-free way in which the last Prime Minister dealt with these questions. I do not say 'addressed' these questions because I do not believe he ever addressed them with the consideration they deserved.

The United States has already held many inquiries into what has gone wrong. One that was not very well publicized was conducted by Ambassador Freeman for the purpose of instructing the newly elected Congressmen at a special seminar after the 2006 elections. We shall not need to have the same thing for new prime ministers, but nevertheless the advice is important. Ambassador Freeman pointed out that the world today is not more dangerous than it was in the Cold War, but it is a good deal less orderly, less predictable and more complex. In those circumstances he pointed out that the defence budget of the United States (last year just over $440 billion, which is more than the defence expenditure of 192 other countries combined) in itself guarantees nothing. He said: 'What we lack is not military might but political acumen. Our failings are not those of muscle but of the mind'. The National Security Council, which steered the United States through the hazards of the Cold War, was unable to make the same impact on recent events. The result of that faces us today in Iran.

Playing into Iran's Hands

It is certainly not an easy task to handle Iran. I had a limited experience of it. We had broken off relations with Iran in

1979, at the same time as the United States, and years of rupture followed thereafter. I was able to bring that detachment to an end first by meeting the Iranian Foreign Minister Ali Akbar Velayati at the United Nations, and then by bringing him to London in February 1989. We actually reached the point of re-establishing relations, only for them to be shattered less than a fortnight later by the fatwa against Salman Rushdie. That kind of hazard indicates the sensitivity of the problems that we face.

The background today is much less auspicious than it was then, because in the name of fighting terrorism – in that broadest and most unhelpful definition of the 'war against terror' – the United States and perhaps we, to some extent, have actually increased the power of Iran. The removal of the Taliban from Afghanistan diminished the threat to Iran from the east. The removal of Saddam Hussein, Iran's deadly enemy to the west, had the same effect. The arrival in Baghdad of an Iran-friendly Shiite government for the first time in history was a third factor, which has virtually ensured the emergence of Iran as a major power centre in the region, rivalled probably only by Israel. Iran appears all the more hostile as a result of the extravagant populist rhetoric of Mr Ahmadinejad, but I have to say, alas, that some of the remarks that come from Washington in response often have the same effect. The oft-repeated statement by Vice-President Cheney that we are in the 'year of Iran' was not a helpful comment on the handling of the future. It was an uncomfortable reminder of the exchanges of rhetoric that preceded the conflict in and attack upon Iraq.

There is a risk that even now, among some of our American friends, military action is no longer regarded as absolutely the last resort, needing the clearest possible justification in accordance with the United Nations charter. The doctrine of pre-emptive strikes and preventive conflict has certainly not been formally abandoned. The distinguished American commentator William Pfaff warned in the *New York Review of Books* against 'world hegemonistic thinking' as being a real 'disservice to American interests'.

We in the United Kingdom must be pretty humble about that as well, because it was once our own habit. There is still a picture at the top of the stairs in the Foreign Office, put up in about 1916, depicting Britannia Bellatrix, which is not the kind of picture that any of us would put on show there today. It took us half a century to learn the lessons of the limitations of Empire, starting in South Africa and going on to Suez. I am afraid that the same kind of learning curve is necessary today.

Finally, where do we go next on the outstanding problems, in particular on Iran? Whether we are addressing the problem of handling Iran or the Israel–Palestine problem, the multilateral approach must be regarded as fundamental. The handling of North Korea, leading to some recent agreement, as far as it goes points the way. It was anything but reassuring to hear the reaction of the former ambassador to the United Nations, John Bolton, saying that such agreement 'sends exactly the wrong signal to would-be proliferators around the world'. I must say, on the contrary, that the constructive involvement of China in particular in those negotiations has had a very positive impact.

The growing importance of China is symbolized by the fact that its current currency reserves, a mountain of gold growing by $200 billion a year, is $1.1 trillion. China's growing maturity is demonstrated by its support for UN resolutions about Iran. I can summarize the significance of being close to China, as well as Russia, our European partners and the United States, in a phrase borrowed from Michael Heseltine. Recently, he said this: 'The growing interdependence of our several self-interests is the glue of future world security'. It is important to recognize this in respect of every possible partner. That is the way in which to approach the Iran problem. What is needed now, in the words of Dr Ian Davis, the Co-executive Director of the British American Security Information Council, is 'smart, tough-minded multilateral diplomacy – of the kind that has just been applied to North

Korea'. It is, he continued, 'not only less risky than military options but also more likely to produce real and long-lasting progress'.

For the United Kingdom, the best way to maximize our influence in that process, as much for the Arab–Israel problem as for the Iran problem, is through our participation in and leadership, as far as we can give it, of the European Union. In that way we are part of the quartet in the Arab–Israel problem and that is the way in which we and other Europeans, alongside the Americans, Russians and Chinese, are all now lined up on the right side of the argument as far as Iran is concerned. That concerted pressure certainly needs to be maintained, but the most useful and vital contribution that the United States can and should make to the conclusion of those negotiations – pace John Bolton – is an unambiguous promise on its part that if Iran returns to compliance with the nuclear rules, it will face no attempt by the United States to overthrow the regime. A clear assurance of that kind, as part of the process, is one of the components of progress that we have to achieve.

5

DOING OUR FIGHTING MEN AND WOMEN JUSTICE

Michael Heseltine

A suitor of relatively limited means who tries to woo two heiresses at the same time risks being rejected by both. But if he chooses one and becomes her trusted and even dominant consort, the other is likely to treat him with respect. The United Kingdom has uneasily tried to straddle the Atlantic for far too long, a deeply ungainly and undignified posture. We are not equidistant between the United States and Europe, as this government seems to believe. We are a part of Europe, but also the US's best friend within Europe.

However much we may criticize many of Europe's institutions – and I have done so with great vigour on such issues as the budget, its over-regulated economy, its bureaucracy and its creeping federalism (see for example my book *The Challenge of Europe*, 1989) – no serious politician in the United Kingdom can advocate our withdrawal from the European Union. The consequences for our economy, our trade and our influence in the world would be catastrophic. Around half of our trade and investment flows are with Europe, the same amount as with the rest of the world put together. That is the real world we live in. It is flat earthism to suggest otherwise.

But our close friendship with the United States is also a huge advantage in defusing unnecessary tensions between the two greatest groupings of democratic peoples in the world. In particular, in the long run, I believe it will greatly help in negotiating the free trade zone so desperately needed between Europe and the United States.

Human institutions, particularly successful ones, take a long time to adjust to changed circumstances. The Cold War, when the world really did face a 'terror' threat (that of the instant annihilation of hundreds of millions of people at the press of a button in a nuclear exchange), ended nearly two decades ago and is as remote to an entire generation of young people as was World War II to those born in 1965. Yet the institutional landscape we inhabit has surprisingly barely altered, as happened dramatically after the 1939–45 conflict. NATO, the EU and the UN remain much the same, if somewhat expanded.

In one sense this is a good thing, because one should proceed cautiously in reforming institutions which have worked well. But more far-reaching and imaginative solutions are called for to deal with the economic challenges posed by the rise of new powers like China, India and Brazil; the great environmental problems such as climate change; the huge issue of global poverty and the grave security problems posed by international terrorism, failed or renegade states in the Middle East and Africa, and by North Korea. I am profoundly optimistic. In addition to the threat of mutual annihilation being lifted, the globe has embarked on a decade of unprecedented prosperity. Short of an unanticipated catastrophe our children can look forward to an even better life than we enjoyed, as we enjoyed a much better one than our own parents.

However, the dearth of forward thinking on defence and security issues has led to a world in which a few unbalanced dictatorships and their terrorist allies dominate the headlines, while the United States has been expected to play the role of world policeman alone – a role that is quite simply too demanding for any one country, even one as big and strong as the United States. I do not share in the US-bashing now more fashionable as a result of the misadventures in Iraq and Afghanistan; the majority of Americans can now see the folly of those adventures, even if it took them longer than many of us. The United States remains a great and resourceful nation and if it has made mistakes in its approach to these difficult problems, it can learn the correct course under new leaders, just as it has done in the past.

There is fault on all sides. The Europeans too often condemn the gung-ho approach of the United States while committing far too little to the more comprehensive security arrangements necessary to preserve the peace. The Americans have been understandably prickly after 9/11, and too often go it alone. I am deeply critical of the foreign policy of the present Bush administration. My criticism is in sharp contrast to my admiration – indeed gratitude – for what I see as a Pax Americana that dominated the second half of the twentieth century. At a great cost the United States preserved a balance of peace in the Pacific, the Middle East and Europe, using its military power of course for its own interests, but greatly to our benefit as well. Just as we gained as a consequence, so we will suffer for more recent misjudgements.

There is always a temptation to call for root-and-branch overhaul of ageing institutions. I urge caution. The United Nations was bound to be more talking shop than active instrument but, for all its frustrations, it serves a valuable purpose. But it has few teeth and I would welcome an initiative to allow the creation of a genuine quasi-military organization for peacekeeping or troubleshooting purposes. Across the world we see tinpot regimes or guerrilla forces act in barbarous circumstances. A United Nations capability recruited like the French Foreign Legion could be a valuable instrument and devoid of the national associations that make it so difficult for democratic governments to deploy troops in apparently irrelevant war zones.

Europe should certainly play a more effective role in its own defence. Without the United States it is difficult to believe that post-war Europe could have resisted Stalin's westward encroachment. NATO has been the essential bulwark of our democratic freedoms. I would argue to keep the United States firmly entrenched on our soil. Our European track record is not encouraging. But I despair at the re-emergence of anti-Russian antagonism. Caution is a legitimate and prudent ingredient of foreign policy, but Russia is a European power. It has much more to gain from co-operation with the West than to lose. NATO and the EU now stretches to its frontiers. That is to be welcomed but, in the dark moments of Russian gloom, they will remember Napoleon and Hitler. It was only 60 years ago.

Meanwhile, what can the United Kingdom contribute today? Our defence and security outlook regrettably presents a sorry spectacle, with the institutions required to make it work being overstretched and run down as the government increasingly resorts to headline grabbing legislation to restrict our liberties. It is no good grandstanding internationally and despatching forces all over the world, or giving the police enhanced powers, if these forces are simultaneously losing the means and morale to carry out their existing tasks.

The United Kingdom's armed forces are amongst the finest and most professional in the world. One of the chief reasons for this is the sense of purpose that they are serving their country and fellow Britons. They do not feel that they are just cannon fodder to be expended on adventures in foreign fields at the whim of governments. In addition, they require continuing financial support that allows them to minimize the risk when they put their lives in danger and that gives them decent training, pay, housing and prospects if they decide to return to civilian life. They must also be assured of the support and respect of their fellow countrymen if they are to be asked to risk their lives on our behalf – the greatest sacrifice one human being can make for another.

Undermining the United Kingdom's
Servicemen and Women

Yet in all these respects British servicemen and women are being severely tried today, although admirably they show no sign of buckling. It is a service that demands loyalty and no speaking out of turn; so it is the duty of others, particularly their political representatives, to do so for them.

To address the first issue: Our service personnel are not allowed to question the cause they are fighting for; and nor had there been any reason to do so when they were fighting not just for country but on the side of all that was right and decent against tyrants from Napoleon to Kaiser Wilhelm to Hitler to Communist proxies. Today – and it is unwise to patronize our service personnel, who are immensely aware, and have access to all modern media – they are much less sure that they are fighting in the United Kingdom's identifiable interests.

Take Afghanistan as an example. In the search for Bin Laden after the outrage in New York, it was a wholly legitimate decision to enter Afghanistan in an attempt to bring him to justice. That decision is very different from the present policy of trying to create a society based on institutions and assumptions that have few historic roots in that country. Take Iraq as an example. Of course Saddam's regime was a wicked one, half a world away from the United Kingdom. That didn't prevent us from relying on its help in the 1980s when Iran was seen as the most significant threat to regional stability.

It would seem irresponsible to suggest an immediate withdrawal, but if matters seem likely only to get worse, if we are seen as taking sides in a deepening sectarian conflict (some of the worst atrocities are being carried out by Shiite militias, often working with the very police and ministers of the government we are upholding), if our soldiers are simply lightning rods for fire from all sides, does it make any sense to go on? It is quite clear that today the situation in Iraq is radically worse than expected when we entered the country in 2003. I never found the justifications for the war credible. If they seemed doubtful at the time they are more so now. The Labour government must accept a share of the blame for having loosened the fearsome hatreds of a society that had been held in the iron grip of a regime of terror and fear. We failed to ask what would happen if the grip was suddenly removed. We created a vacuum into which new poisons immediately flowed. It was predictable and predicted.

If we can save many lives by our continuing presence, it would indeed be irresponsible to withdraw precipitately. But if on the contrary it is a matter of our own soldiers losing their precious lives in a hopelessly deepening civil war, if our presence there as an army of occupation perceived to be in league with one side (the Shiites) is actually making matters worse, we have to ask why should we seek such a supreme sacrifice from our fellow countrymen, and for what? Unhappily, to feel that they are out on a limb on a hopeless and thankless mission will truly undermine the spirit of our fighting men and the effectiveness of our army. Armies in a democracy should be asked to fight where there is public support for the cause for which they fight. In neither the United States nor this country is that the case.

Moreover our soldiers are ill-equipped, in terms of modern weaponry and protection, on the battlefield. On the basic issue of manpower, the number of those we have sent to fight overseas wars in recent years has stretched our limited resources to breaking point. On equipment, stories abound of the way in which our men in the field are being failed by their political masters. Equipment is improvised, there are spare parts shortages and there are shortages of essential armour and body protection.

General Freddie Viggers, the Adjutant-General, recently highlighted the way the Ministry of Defence is failing to provide adequate accommodation for soldiers both before they leave for the battlefield and on their return, and their families.

The army Chief of Staff, General Sir Richard Dannatt, has declared that the United Kingdom's presence in Iraq is exacerbating the security problems there. General Sir Michael Rose has attacked the insouciance of a Prime Minister holidaying while British soldiers are facing a winter of unprecedented risk and hardship in Iraq and Afghanistan. General Sir Michael Jackson has made much the same point. General Richard Sherriff has complained that wounded soldiers do not receive adequate treatment when they return home.

Pleas by service chiefs for more money are a standard feature of pre-budget manoeuvring. But the clamour this time is deafening. The price has been deteriorating equipment, less protection for our soldiers as they experience greater risk, and service pay dropping significantly behind that in other comparable sections of society – a quarter of the army earns less than £25,000 a year; some 40% live in unsatisfactory accommodation. In 2004-5 the shortfall in recruiting tripled, although it recovered a little the following year. There is still an overall shortfall of 1,500 soldiers. In an MOD survey nearly a quarter of service personnel wanted to leave at the earliest possible opportunity. More than 1,000 service personnel have gone missing since the start of the Iraq war. At the same time the MOD has announced plans to spend £2.3 billion on new offices, including chairs for more than 3,000 civil servants costing £1,000 each and 3,500 oak doors at £1,200 each, with a luxurious marble and stone floor for the building.

I am not one of those who believe the United Kingdom should find the money by sacrificing its independent nuclear deterrent. The cost, spread out over many years, is in my view acceptable and necessary to allowing us freedom to make our own defence decisions. But if British forces are going to be required to undertake a much bigger continuing role abroad – a reality today, although in my view the case for it has been far from proven – it is obvious they must be properly equipped and paid.

Defence in a Changing United Kingdom

There are other, less obvious problems for the armed forces in today's rapidly changing society. British troops are being used increasingly for a variety of non-military tasks, such as peace-keeping, distributing aid, minor reconstruction and winning over the locals through good works. This is admirable, but they need the resources to do all these different things.

The armed forces are under increasingly intense scrutiny on issues of bullying, sexism and racism, rightly so, but this should not detract from their ability to carry out their military duties. Legal challenges to the armed forces have become more frequent, and in a recent MOD survey some 60% of personnel expressed dissatisfaction about how they are handled. Under its armed forces bill the government has restricted the power of commanding officers to dismiss charges against their soldiers – an unwarranted slur on the professional abilities of senior officers, and further complicating these processes and possibly even leading to political interference. Soldiers have become increasingly reluctant to open fire in dangerous situations for fear of 'subsequent investigation'. Servicemen and women and their families, feeling abandoned by their superiors in the government, have become more disposed to enter into litigation.

Much of this is a result of the way society itself has been changing. But it is clear that the old deference of soldiers, however professional, towards their commanders cannot be taken for granted – especially if there is intense controversy among the British people about the nature of the mission they are risking their lives for. Servicemen and women watch television and read newspapers just like anyone else; they need to be convinced of the rightness of their cause, not merely be ordered to follow orders blindly. If military ventures appear to be undertaken at the Prime Minister's whim, with expendable personnel on combat missions that do not clearly seem to be in vital national interests, and if in addition they feel inadequately protected, paid and housed, the effect on the morale and the effectiveness of our fighting forces could be devastating. It is the painstakingly acquired body of institutional loyalty and professionalism that this government has imperilled.

What are the solutions?

1. The first suggests itself. A much more rigorous and considered approach to further deployment of our armed forces in war zones is needed. Above all, service personnel want to feel that they are serving British national interests, and that British public opinion stands foursquare behind them. This consideration should lead us seriously to consider calling for a withdrawal from both Iraq and Afghanistan. It is not in the national interest badly to weaken our armed forces solely to 'keep the Americans company' when they go to war.

2. If – and the case is far from proven, rather the reverse – the United Kingdom's armed forces are increasingly to be despatched into combat situations abroad, then inevitably military spending will have to rise accordingly. There is no such thing as war on the cheap.

3. As Defence Secretary, I introduced the amalgamation of service commands at the top that permitted a much more efficient, militarily effective and cost-efficient approach to joint military operations. In addition, through my MINIS system of departmental accountability, I was able to achieve significant reductions in the civilian staff of the MOD. There are still substantial savings to be made. The bottom line is that the front line must take priority over bureaucratic lines in the rear.

   Servicemen have selflessly put aside the trade unionism of civil society out of loyalty to their country. The government must show awareness of this sacrifice and reward them accordingly. Already we have the formation of Military Families Against the War in Iraq, the Army Rumour Service on the internet and, most ominously of all, the proposal for a British Armed Forces Federation, which would have a potentially disastrous effect. This is the result of the cavalier negligence towards our brave men and women in uniform currently practised over the past few years by the government.

4. I also opened up the MOD's defence procurement to greatly increased competitive tendering. We must remove the temptation to slip back into cosy arrangements between the MOD and the armaments industry.

5. We need greater exchanges between the cost-conscious and more effective private sector and the MOD. This is not to be confused with the injection of capital to build the new MOD headquarters, for example, under the Private Finance Initiative, which in the right hands can work well and in the wrong hands can allow government departments to offload huge amounts of debt from their books and flout public spending targets.

6. Finally, defence procurement across Europe still remains lamentably national-based. This is an area in which the United Kingdom can press for much closer European co-operation. If the American defence industry were organized at state level, defence needs and equipment would be analysed and equipment designed in 50 different programmes, reflecting the interests of each state's industrial base. No such nightmare of inefficiency exists on that side of the Atlantic, but it does on the British side. That was why the Inter European Programme Group (IEPG) was set up in 1976, consisting of all the European members of the NATO alliance, including France.

For the United Kingdom, as one of the largest European producers of military equipment, there were and remain two broad issues. The first is the near impossibility of maintaining a national manufacturing capability for every type of defence equipment. The cost of research and development of each major weapon is constantly increasing, and the production runs necessary to supply the British armed forces alone are small and therefore relatively expensive. Some of the Ministry of Defence's suppliers (British Aerospace and Rolls Royce, for example) are monopoly suppliers, although competing on a world stage.

The second consideration behind the formation of the IEPG was that, while chances of agreeing common specifications and accepting the need to share costs may be remote, the procurement policies of the US – rigorously scrutinized by Congress – ensure that American taxpayers' money is spent in the United States. Only where a European manufacturer has achieved a technological breakthrough which makes his product uniquely attractive to the American armed services will his company be likely to secure a contract. There is a dilemma. How can American co-operation with Europe be balanced when the small companies and small procurement programmes of European countries face gigantic equivalents on the other side of the Atlantic? Co-operation within the Atlantic alliance is very desirable, but genuine co-operation will come only when Europe can co-ordinate its resources and bring them into the common pool.

Since the IEPG was set up in 1976, the separate national bureaucracies of Europe have continued to maintain their separate national procurement systems. There has been too little effective challenge. In its first seven years, the IEPG members never met at ministerial level and the research directors met only by chance – too late to discover whose work was being wastefully duplicated by whom. There was no overall strategy, no clear set of options, nothing but a vocal enthusiasm, oft-repeated, for European defence co-operation. Progress is not impossible as the Tornado programme and then the European Fighter Aircraft proved, but it requires determined ministerial commitment.

In 1984, as Secretary of State for Defence, I, together with my Dutch colleague State Secretary for Defence Van Howelingen (at that time chairman of IEPG), decided to upgrade the work of the IEPG, convinced as we were that unless we Europeans could learn to work consistently together, in competition but to common specifications, the value of Europe's research and development effort could never match that of the Americans, directed by the Pentagon and by NASA, or of the MITI-sponsored Japanese programmes. I was determined that senior defence ministers should attend IEPG discussions, and with some difficulty this was achieved.

* * *

Let me conclude by quoting the military covenant by which the British nation solemnly promises that it will look after the needs of servicemen and women in exchange for their loyalty and sacrifice:

> Soldiers will be called upon to make personal sacrifices – including the ultimate sacrifice – in the service of the Nation. In putting the needs of the Nation and the Army before their own, they forgo some of the rights enjoyed by those outside the Armed Forces. In return, British soldiers must always be able to expect fair treatment, to be valued and respected as individuals, and that they (and their families) will be sustained and rewarded by commensurate terms and conditions of service. In the same way, the unique nature of military land operations means that the Army differs from all other institutions, and must be sustained and provided for accordingly by the Nation. This mutual obligation forms the Military Covenant between the Nation, the Army and each individual soldier; an unbreakable common bond of identity, loyalty and responsibility which has sustained

the Army and its soldiers throughout its history.
It has perhaps its greatest manifestation in the annual
commemoration of Armistice Day, when the Nation
keeps covenant with those who have made the ultimate
sacrifice, giving their lives in action.

6

UNITING OUR ENEMIES AND DIVIDING OUR FRIENDS

Zbigniew Brzezinski

Let me begin by asking a simple question. Do the United States and Europe today share a jointly defined purpose? Do we partake of the same interpretation of the essence of the challenge that our new times, the post-Cold War times, pose to us?

Last year President Bush made an important attempt to define both the purpose and the meaning of what we face. In his speech, he compared the war on terrorism to the Cold War. He felt there were significant historical analogies between these two phenomena, that are helpful in understanding both our purpose and the nature of our times. With due respect to the President, I have an uneasy feeling about some of the formulations involved, beginning with his definition of the challenge, 'we're fighting the followers of a murderous ideology that despises freedom', and continuing with his definition of the threat, 'they're seeking weapons of mass destruction, which means they would pose a threat to the United States as great as the Soviet Union'. In my opinion, his definition of the challenge is too vague, and his definition of the threat is too sweeping.

There are risks in definitions that are too vague or too sweeping. The vagueness of the President's statement of the challenge runs the risk of unintentionally uniting our enemies while dividing our friends. This is the very opposite of what we did in the early years of the Cold War, when we strove to unite our friends and to divide our enemies. And we ought to be particularly careful if our definition of the enemy is too vague but by implication too all-embracing – it might unite the world of Islam against both the United States and Europe.

The definition of the nature of the threat is also too sweeping, because while the threat is serious in the long run, it is still minor compared to what the Soviet Union posed. Looking back for a minute to my own experience in the White House, part of my job was to inform the President that we were under nuclear attack. We could not exclude that possibility, and at times we were worried about it. I had roughly three minutes in which to verify the nature of the attack and its scale, which would involve several progressive steps. The President, once I reached him, would have four minutes to decide how to respond depending on the scale of the attack. Then the execution would be set in motion. Six hours later, approximately 160 million people would be dead. I think it's important to have the distinction between the overwhelming threat of the Cold War and today's terrorist threat in mind because exaggeration of a threat is liable to produce only excessive fear.

Some might say that deterrence worked, that we won the Cold War. But at the time there was no certainty. And in addition to that, there was always a chance of a mishap, of a technical glitch, of a war by miscalculation. I submit that the danger the terrorists might acquire nuclear weapons some day from one, two or conceivably three nuclear powers is not as high as those risks. And indeed it is not so high because increasingly we know that nuclear forensics will identify the source of the weapon, and thus deterrence can be applicable for destruction of the source of that weapon. Moreover, the use of one or two or three weapons, while horrendous to contemplate given current circumstances, is still nothing compared to 160 million people dead in six hours.

It is important to have a sense of proportion, which helps to understand the problems we face. I do not feel that we have either a national or a transatlantic consensus about the nature of the challenge we confront or about the nature of the danger we face. We had that consensus at the time of the Atlantic Charter, and we need it today. What we need today is a shared understanding of the things that make our time unique. That understanding must recognize what is unique both about the world in general and about the particular threat we face.

Let me make a stab, just a stab, at a formulation. On the general level, what is distinctive about our time is that the United States and Europe, the most advanced part of the world, face a massive and unprecedented global political awakening. That is something new in all of history. The world as a whole is experiencing today what French society as a whole experienced during the French Revolution – a sudden stirring of political awareness, unleashed passions, fermenting excitement and escalating aspirations. Today that sense of revolution is the political reality worldwide and it is altogether new, though it has been developing over a number of decades.

Today, even in remote Nepal, Bolivia and Kyrgyzstan, we see similar manifestations of political behaviour. Today in Somalia, East Timor and Chechnya we see similar manifestations of brutal violence. And throughout the world we see similar trends in the rise of radical populism, which carries with it the potential for violent extremism. This radical populism, organized through the internet and fuelled by the images of human inequality that are disseminated globally by the electronic media, is also stimulated by a new political reality. This political reality is no longer that of an aroused peasantry or that of the industrial proletariat of Marx; it is some 120 million fermenting and politically active university students throughout the world. That is the new reality we confront together, and it is a much more complex and difficult reality than we faced during the Cold War, World War I or World War II.

On the more specific level we are facing the reality of radical populism increasingly in the form of extremist Islamic fundamentalism. This specific political reality can be geographically described – it operates largely in that part of the world which I have referred to as 'the global Balkans', which essentially extends from Suez to Sichuan. It is a part of the world that has faced and become increasingly aroused at foreign intrusion. This was the case in Afghanistan in response to the Soviet invasion, and this is now the case in the Persian Gulf in response to the American invasion.

This increasingly resentful and extremist fundamentalism uses terrorism to compensate for its technological weakness. This strategy is known as asymmetrical warfare, and its use is widespread. We should recognize the expanding potential for this danger in Afghanistan, a nation traditionally hostile to outsiders that is becoming increasingly xenophobic. What has prevented Afghanistan's hostility from erupting against us is the fact that we helped Afghanistan. Consequently many Afghans still view us as their allies, but their numbers are decreasing.

This violent fundamentalism is also expressed by anticolonialism in Iraq because, for the Iraqis who dislike our occupation, our presence is an unpleasant reminder of their colonial past. And this new political reality involves intensifying hostility with Iran, instability in Pakistan and the continued mistreatment of Palestine. All of these critical situations pose the danger of American engagement in a fermenting and increasingly violent region of approximately 550 million people.

Transatlantic Dialogue

We need, therefore, a transatlantic dialogue about the nature of our time, about the new aspects of the dilemmas we face, and about what we can do together concerning these general and specific challenges. That dialogue requires two sides. It requires an atlanticist United States that respects Europe and recognizes its own need for counsel and support. And it requires a political Europe that realizes that its global responsibilities are not only socio-economic, but that the world needs a Europe that also has the political and military capacity to act jointly with the United States.

In recent years the United States has veered away from the centrality of the American–European connection in world affairs. At the same time the European Union, which was emerging as a political union when Europe was still divided in half, has been evolving into a European Community since Europe became whole and free. That itself is a paradox, because the apt name for what exists today is the European Community and what existed until 1990 was in fact a nascent European Union.

We can only have a transatlantic dialogue when there are strategically minded interlocutors speaking for Europe as a whole, not when they are speaking for individual national positions, as was the case during the initial phase of the Iraq war. When Prime Minister Blair whispered to us sound advice (which we accepted but rarely heeded) while publicly endorsing what we did, when Chancellor Schroeder disassociated himself from us for domestic political reasons and when President Chirac did the same for reasons of historical nostalgia, our international dialogue failed.

The United States has an obligation to listen when Europe as a whole speaks to us. Perhaps the European team involving Merkel, Brown and Sarkozy, backed by Prodi, Zapatero and Kaczynski, can again formulate a European perspective that the United States will be forced to recognize. To arrive at that point of co-operation we must cultivate our dialogue and move forward on several issues of common concern, thereby creating opportunities not only for joint action but for shared perspective as well.

I sense in Europe a realization that there is an absence of leadership. And the realization of a negative condition is the beginning of the resolution of that condition. I think there is a growing consensus in Europe that the Europeans have to work together and, while a common perspective on world affairs must involve all 25 European states, in reality the opinions of some countries are more important than the opinions of others. Six countries are particularly important and, in that sense, there is already an opportunity for an informal dialogue and a shared perception. From an American point of view, I believe that forging this European consensus is essential.

Consensus is essential for Europe's unity, but it is also essential for us if we are to be effective in the global scene. The United States needs solid European counsel to avoid unrealistic views of the world. September 11th established a tendency towards self-isolation in American society by stoking domestic fear, spreading undefined anxieties and revealing enemies that could not be precisely defined. In order to remove ourselves from this isolation we must seek a partner in our rapidly changing world. Europe is that partner. I think the Europeans themselves realize that if the United States is to be a constructive player in international affairs, Europe must support us and interact with us with the kind of vision that we shared at the beginning of the Cold War and during World War II.

Military power is essential but secondary. Even though 9/11 has caused the United States to take a decidedly military approach to foreign affairs, the solution to the new problems we face cannot be purely military. We need an American–European-led international effort to improve the quality of global institutions in order to forestall the world's growing inequality. This inequality is not only economic disparity in the most tangible sense, but also cultural inequality, the inequality of sophistication and understanding which creates friction and culture wars. Solving this problem will require wisdom beyond that which was necessary to win the past wars that confronted the United States and Europe. But Churchill and Roosevelt did not just concentrate on winning World War II. Their message went beyond winning the war; their alliance was about the kind of world that would be built in the aftermath of the conflict.

Our problem is more complicated than that which confronted our ancestors; our challenge is more difficult. But it is now a global challenge, and the Europeans and we are the people who must respond to it. The Chinese might some day be struck by radical populism. If so, I hope they do not attempt to become leaders of that hostile global movement. Knowing their sense of self-interest and their commercial orientation, I would predict that they will not do so, but if we fail to solidify the transatlantic alliance even that could happen.

Joint initiatives can also contribute to an Atlantic grand consensus. There are four areas in which I think joint movement is timely, necessary and possible. I will not attempt to prescribe policies, but allow me to suggest some general principles.

The Middle East

Firstly, in the region of the Middle East and the Persian Gulf, our emphasis should be not on coercion but on consensus. Specifically, we need to engage Iran. I was gratified to hear the decision taken by the United States to participate jointly with key European interlocutors in shaping a new proposal to Iran, offering it, putting it forward, and then negotiating it if the Iranians respond in a constructive fashion. I hope this initiative moves forward. I think it was a timely gesture as well as a courageous one by this administration, given the fact that the President's opposition to this type of approach is widely known. I feel that the initiative is both timely and potentially positive.

I am concerned about the tone in which the Iran proposal was packaged, however, because that could benefit Iranian extremists who do not want negotiations and who want to use confrontation as the basis for consolidating their position. I hope that we will be patient enough, even if the initial Iranian responses are not positive, to pursue this approach.

That requires time, and I think we should recognize the fact that the Iranian problem, while serious, is not urgently imminent. We have time to deal with it intelligently and we have taken the right step. American participation is essential.

Iran is containable, in the sense that it is contained right now. Whether it is contained because we have imposed limits that it does not dare to cross or whether it does not have the aspiration to cross these limits, I'm not sure I know. What I do know is that Iran is a serious country. It is not a country created at Versailles or shortly thereafter by western statesmen with pencils in their hands, but one with a historical identity and a sense of its worth and imperial tradition. It is one of the six or eight truly historic nations in the world, and you sense that reality when you talk to leaders of these nations. There is something specific, deeper and broader about them.

It is also a country which was hesitantly, ambiguously, but gradually moving towards democracy until the deterioration in American–Iranian relations aborted that process several years ago. It is also a country which, if you look at social-educational indices, has the best chance of any Muslim country, after Turkey, of evolving into a democracy. Iran has a level of education, a degree of literacy and a role for women in society that is outstanding in the Muslim world. The number of women in Iranian universities is greater than men, there are a large number of women in the professions, and there is even an elected female vice president – something in the US we still don't have! I think Iran has a chance of evolving. I welcome the offer of talks, assuming it moves forward, assuming that it wasn't offered on a confrontational basis and assuming we make real progress, because I am inclined to be relatively optimistic about the role of Iran in an extremely volatile part of the world in which established and firm political entities are still questionable. The more we can normalize our relationship with Iran and the longer we can postpone the moment of truth on the nuclear issue, the better, because I think time is on our side.

Secondly, regarding the Israeli–Palestinian peace process, I believe we must clearly define our ultimate objective. The two parties to the conflict are very suspicious of each other. Until they see the outline of an eventual settlement and until that settlement is articulated and supported both by the United States and Europe, suspicions will predominate and reluctance to make concessions will remain strong. Both Palestinian and Israeli public opinions today, according to polls, are ahead of their governments in willingness to compromise. This applies both on the territorial issue and on the issue of Jerusalem. A joint American–European declaration of the basic principles upon which the peace settlement ought to be based would accelerate the peace process and galvanize moderate public opinion.

Thirdly, in Iraq, we have to make a break with notions of tutelage, which evoke memories of Iraq's colonial past. Talk of Iraq's incapacity for self-government and discussion of an indefinite American military presence in Iraq to forestall civil war is neglectful of history. It reminds me of the discussions in France regarding Algeria before President de Gaulle abandoned this refrain and realized that the French presence in Algeria was not only harming France but was perpetuating the conflict itself. We must recognize that the Iraqis are no longer living in the colonial age, that they are a sophisticated people with the capacity to govern themselves and that they have the ability to resolve their civil strife more effectively than an occupation army. Their solution may be more brutal than ours, but we do not have the capacity to resolve the problem decisively and our continued presence will only perpetuate the conflict.

Finally, in the Middle East regarding democratization – we should first focus not on elections but on human rights. Human rights enshrine the rule of law and develop the electoral process, eventually producing democracy. Elections are the last stage in the process of democratization. Insisting on immediate democracy in an era and region in which radical populism is particularly strong is an unwise and self-destructive policy.

I could envisage, for example, an American or NATO presence in the territories of an independent Palestinian state, working to provide for demilitarization and security. I can see, after the termination of the current American presence in Iraq, a continued American presence in Kuwait. I can see some arrangements for a residual military presence in Kurdistan as part of a united Iraq, in order to discourage the neighbours who feel particularly neuralgic about Kurdish autonomy. There are a number of ways such a presence can be defined in addition to air bases and naval facilities, but I think that the ones I have mentioned are the primary ones. Of course, if we stumble into some sort of a military conflict with Iran, we won't have much choice. We will have to be militarily present in Iraq, Iran, Afghanistan and even Pakistan if it explodes. If that process begins to escalate, then the United States will be entrenched in the 'global Balkans' for the next 20 years, and American global primacy will be permanently lost.

Russia, NATO, India and China

The second large issue for a transatlantic consensus involves Russia. Russia must be neither isolated nor propitiated. The United States cannot abandon its attendance at the G8, but we should be prepared to use that platform to discuss Russia's stifling of democracy, including its intervention in Moldova and its support for separatism in Georgia. We should ask why Russia refuses to ratify the energy charter between itself and the European Union, which is important to energy security. Inviting Russia to become part of our community by meeting international obligations is the right mode of engagement.

We must pursue a strategy based on a sense of history. If Ukraine sustains its independence and begins to join NATO and the EU, it would be a catalyst for Russia to follow suit. Poland and the Baltic republics are too alien to the Russians to have encouraged Russia to follow them. But a democratic Ukraine which becomes increasingly a part of the European family is going to have a contagious impact on Russia. This could open the door to Russia becoming increasingly associated with Europe, which is in the long-term interest of Russia and also in the interest of the Atlantic world.

Energy is an issue the Europeans and we ought to discuss seriously with the Russians. Ultimately it is also an issue in which a constructive approach is not only in our interest but also in the interest of the Russians, not just economically, but politically. Although the Russians may be drunk with dollars right now and call themselves a great energy world power, they're missing a very important point – they occupy a huge space that is becoming increasingly empty. They're dying. They're getting drunk. Their lives are getting shorter. And they're leaving the Far East.

Russia needs to be more closely related to the West so that there is investment not just in Russian energy but in Russian economic development. We have here an immediate agenda that we need to address. Beyond that, I think if it were possible to do something akin to the Manhattan Project on a transatlantic basis, undertaking it would be in our mutual interest. I think both the Europeans and the United States have a long-term interest in somewhat reducing our dependency on oil. I deliberately use the word 'somewhat', because the notion of eliminating dependency on oil is (i) unrealistic and (ii) uneconomical. The more we reduce our dependency on oil, the more the price will go down. The more the price goes down, the more economical it is to use oil. That particular problem cannot be resolved. But I think a Manhattan project by the Americans and the Europeans together, involving nuclear energy or fuel cells or other new technologies, may be beneficial. It would be an objective that both the American population and the European population would endorse, and it would be a signal to others that the free ride on exorbitant oil prices is going to come to an end.

It might also stimulate the Russians to stop emulating what the Saudis (and even worse the Nigerians) have been doing with oil profits, and encourage them to start emulating the Norwegians instead. The former export their oil profits to Cyprus, the Cayman Islands and elsewhere. The Norwegians have been using oil revenue to develop comprehensive plans for social transformation and modernization. The Russians have failed in doing that, and I see no reason why in the privacy of St Petersburg we can't tell Putin: 'You need to become serious about this money'. Right now it's flowing either to the West or just to Moscow and St Petersburg – the rest of Russia is stagnating and depopulating. Therefore we have a powerful argument in the immediate future with Russia. We have the opportunity to do something like the Manhattan Project with our European friends to insure our joint energy security.

Modernizing NATO

Thirdly, with regard to NATO, the Atlantic community must rely on a principle not of regionalism but of globalism. Although NATO started as a regional undertaking, neither the United States nor Europe is primarily concerned today with just regional self-defence. The world is now a collective concern, and responsibility for global stability engages both the United States and Europe. For this reason, the gradual expansion of NATO's scope is inevitable and implies increasingly global undertakings. The Dutch government and the Dutch General Secretary of NATO have recently explored the possibility of extending involvement to New Zealand, Australia and Japan. I believe this process should be pursued in the interest of the expanding role of the Atlantic Alliance on the global scale.

The issue of some form of military collaboration with India is a very delicate one. While there are merits to the proposition of a strategic partnership, one has to recognize that there are some negative consequences of that relationship. A military partnership with India could have negative effects on our relationship with Pakistan, which is quite critical to the stabilization of Afghanistan and even Pakistan itself, and also on our relationship with China. These are two significant complications that will impede the expansion of the security relationship between India and the United States. The Indians recognize this themselves.

Even the US's current strategic relationship with India holds the potential for danger. One aspect, for example, of the arrangement we recently made with India which is troublesome to me is that the Indians will now have eight reactors entirely free to pursue the production of nuclear weapons. This in turn means they will be able to produce 50 nuclear weapons a year. Over five years that's 250 nuclear weapons – a sizeable nuclear arsenal. This is troubling because the Chinese, who 41 years ago acquired the capability to produce nuclear weapons, have so far maintained a position of minimal strategic deterrence. Their total arsenal aimed at the United States today is still only about 18 ICBMs. They might not maintain that position if their neighbour and rival, India, begins rapidly to increase its supply of nuclear weapons. An increase in India's strength, therefore, impedes on our own security vis-à-vis China which, for the moment at least, does not pose a serious nuclear threat to the United States.

China

Finally, regarding China, the Atlantic world should recognize that collision is not inevitable. Analogies between China and imperial Germany prior to 1914 are misplaced for two key reasons. At that time, the great powers were not part of an interwoven, interdependent community. We all, including China, increasingly are. Whether we are connected by the WTO, financial flows or energy interdependence, even major powers today arc less independent than was the case with imperial Germany in 1914.

The second reason is more prosaic but just as important. In 1914, most Germans were poor and young. The Chinese are becoming richer and older. By 2020, there will be 250 million Chinese over the age of 65. If handled appropriately, China will not become a revolutionary country. We have to be very careful to avoid a self-fulfilling paranoia about China's rise; though it is a regional power, barring a failure to address China appropriately, it will not become a global power for a long time, and before that occasion arrives we can increasingly interweave it into the international system.

To conclude, when the United States and Europe are united, when we act on the basis of a shared geopolitical perspective, when we define our policies by genuine consensus, when we are motivated not by fear but by historical confidence, there is literally nothing we cannot do. That is what the Atlantic Charter was all about.

7

TRADITIONALISTS VS TRANSFORMATIONISTS

Brent Scowcroft

The world of the Cold War and that which followed its demise so quickly were almost the polar opposites of each other. The Cold War was marked by an apocalyptic threat to us all – if we made a serious mistake, we could literally blow up the world. But it was also, in part perhaps because of that, a relatively tidy world. We knew who the enemy was. We knew what the problems were. It was sometimes difficult to mobilize ourselves to do what needed to be done. But it was an orderly world and both sides knew that any wild adventure could get out of control. So we knew what the problem was and we knew how to go about dealing with it.

Suddenly that world was gone, and in its place was a world without the nuclear threat hanging over us but with a hundred, a thousand little problems. Not huge problems but little problems, vexatious problems, coming out of nowhere. Who would have thought, for example, that the source of an attack on the United States would come from Afghanistan? It seems almost incomprehensible. This is an adjustment that we have had to make. But that's not all. The end of the Cold War, I think, also marked the end of World War I. Not of World

War II, but of World War I. Because the world of 1914 was marked by great optimism and scientific enquiry; man had now become more rational, wars were absurd, we would not have any more wars. Then came World War I, and out of World War I came many of the problems that have vexed us ever since, including the growth of ideologies to order mankind – whether it was Fascism, Nazism or Communism. With the end of the Cold War the last of them, Communism, was given a quiet burial and nobody worried about them any more.

This period also marked the collapse of the last of the world's great empires, another thing we tend to forget. If you look at one of the areas of greatest instability in the world it goes from the Balkans down to the Middle East and into central Asia. Look at the last of the world's empires – the Austro-Hungarian Empire in the Balkans, the Ottoman Empire in the Middle East and the Russian or Soviet Empire in central Asia. Those people freed from empire are still trying to figure out who they are, who they belong to, what is the right way to organize; and they are still in turmoil. Of course, many of these changes didn't happen because of the end of the Cold War. It was a curious conjunction of many forces and a lot of these were very gradual in coming, and simply apparent after the threat of the Soviet Union disappeared. So we are living in a world undergoing fundamental readjustment, beset by the forces that I have described and also other equally fundamental forces or changes in the environment.

What are some of these additional forces? There are a large number, but let me mention just three that I consider most basic. The first is the nature of war. For certainly the last century and before, when you said 'war' the term was understood to mean conflict between states or conflict among states. That form of conflict may be at least for a generation or so passé. Now when you talk about war and conflict it mostly takes place inside states, in civil war or even between state and non-state actors, a very different kind of conflict. This change is occurring at the very time when we, at least in the United States, are priding ourselves on transforming our military establishment into the most efficient machine we have ever had. Its role was to fight on the north German plain. Instead we find ourselves going house to house in the grubbiest, dirtiest, most fundamental kind of conflict. Further, I think the use of the term 'war' as in 'war on terror' may put in our minds inappropriate mental frameworks for thinking about the present threat that we face from terrorism.

The second one of these forces is the distribution of power in the world. Perhaps not since the Roman Empire has any one state had the military and economic power possessed by the United States at the end of the Cold War. This really occurred in 1945, not in 1990, with the defeat of the axis of great powers and the exhaustion of the United Kingdom. But all of this was masked by the Cold War and the perceived temporary great power equal status between the United States and the Soviet Union. The United States is not used to being in this position. For most of our 200-year history, we were not leaders in the formulation of policy in the world. Secure behind our two oceans we ordinarily sat back and waited until the great powers of Europe had set the stage, and then we would decide whether we wanted to join or whether we wanted to stand aside. We weren't the framers, we weren't the formulators, we were the followers. All of a sudden we are on centre stage by ourselves. We really are still trying to figure out what it means to try to formulate what it is you want the world to look at. Not only are we not used to it, but the rest of the world is not used to it.

There is a natural hostility to the big guy on the block. You want to see him taken down a peg, you want to see him humbled and torn. That's a human reaction, but in addition to that, and I think partly because of our behaviour, the United States is no longer getting the benefit of the doubt. My sense is that the rest of the world used to think we mess up all the time in foreign policy, but we mean well. Now, most of the world no longer thinks we mean well, and that's a terrible loss of advantage that has to be recovered somehow.

The third of these forces is that much overworked term, globalization. It is perhaps the most fundamental force in the world today, and it affects us in ways we don't even think about. National borders are eroding. Capital flows dwarf the ability of people to control them. Health can no longer be dealt with by the nation-state itself. It goes across borders. You can have a world epidemic in 24 hours given our transportation system. No country can hope to deal with environmental problems by itself. Commerce is worldwide now in a way that it never was. Most fundamental of all is information technology. We have now politicized the people of the world. For most of man's history the average person maybe knew what was happening in his own village and the neighbouring village, but not much else. He didn't care. That was his world, so he wasn't engaged by the great events of empire and so on. He just went about his business. Now almost everyone in the world is within reach of a television set and so they know what's going on the moment it happens. They react. They react with envy, love, happiness, hate, anger, resentment. You name it. I'm not saying that's the cause of the kind of terrorism we have now. But it certainly exacerbates it. So we're dealing with a different kind of world population.

In addition, in commerce for example, the international corporation until a few years ago tended to be vertically oriented. The corporation did everything that had to be done in order to produce the products that it made. Now the world corporation tends to be horizontally organized. They reach here for this sub-assembly, they reach here for services, so that the corporation is really the assembler and marketer and the world produces the product. That is much more efficient than previously and it is adding to the world's wealth. But it produces great disparities inside nations' borders. The United States is facing that right now where corporate balance sheets are just great but the workers (the hourly workers) are not getting their share. So what's the answer? Terrorism, of course, is a luddite solution to the problem.

Those are the kinds of things that we are trying to grapple with. Globalization also makes the governance of small states more difficult than it already was, because weak states are unable to cope with forces that overwhelm them. That leads, for example, to political atomization. One of the best examples is Yugoslavia – a small state in the Balkans which is now six tiny states. It makes no sense in the world today. Globalization forces are bringing the world together but also leading to political atomization. It encourages drug cartels, which have a free rein in states unable to control their borders, communications, money flows and so on, which are consequent from them. And it also, of course, encourages terrorism. To me globalization is analogous to industrialization 200 years ago. When industrialization came along it really built the modern nation-state, because the state grew in order to control this great industrial behemoth – labour unions, capital flows and all the kinds of things that created the federal regulatory state. Now globalization is having the same effect, but in the opposite direction. The nation-state can no longer do these things. What's the answer? The answer is increasing co-operation, and that leads us to international organization.

The Need to Transform Cold War Institutions

All of this results in a very chaotic world; difficult to predict, difficult to manage. It's almost as if somebody took the lid off the world at the end of the Cold War and inside is this boiling stew. Furthermore, we are trying to cope with this world with the habits of mind and the institutions that were formed during the Cold War. The Cold War was all-consuming for all of us. It pervaded our lives. We built our institutions to cope with it. We built our processes to cope with it. Now it is gone, but not the thought processes.

Within the United States a number of these are obvious. Our Defence Department built a great machine just at the time that the machine was no longer applicable to the most frequent kind of conflict today. Our Intelligence community was formed in 1947, and when it was formed we formed the CIA and the FBI. The CIA was to do intelligence work overseas and the FBI domestically, and they were not to mix. This didn't matter during the Cold War because all of our intelligence problems were overseas. With terrorism it matters greatly. Passing information between two organizations is difficult when they don't like each other and when their methods of operation are diametrically opposed to each other. It's a real problem. That's what we are trying to cope with now. All of our intelligence communities are trying to make the change from focussing on a single target – the Soviet Union about which we knew a great deal – to a hundred targets, some of which we don't even know are targets until something bad happens.

Then there is NATO, a marvellous military instrument. It is the first alliance really able to fight together usefully. But what is it for? The purpose for which it was founded is likely never to be called upon. So what can we do with this great military instrument in the world today that is useful?

The last example is the United Nations. It should be the beneficiary of globalization. But the UN was built in 1945. It had 51 members and they were all the same kind of countries. They all had traditions, they had ways of doing things. In a sense it was a club – a community. Now there are 192 members. The bulk of the new members were not states, and many of them were colonies of the 51 founders. They have very different views about the world, what the world ought to look like and how it ought to be run. So the UN is now a very different organization. The Security Council was set up to solve the problems of the League of Nations where there was no executive authority. Instead you make the permanent members the great powers of the world – and they were in

1945 – and remarkably they're still great powers; but they don't represent the great powers of the world today that need to get together to deal with world problems.

There is another problem with the United Nations – it was built on the sovereign independence of its members. Article 2 says that nothing within the charter shall give the UN the right to interfere in matters essentially within the domestic jurisdiction of states. Since that was written we have had genocide conventions and other kinds of conventions. There is a generally understood responsibility to protect on the part of the UN when a state either cannot or will not provide protection to major elements of its population. Those two principles are in direct conflict with each other, and one of the outcomes right now is Darfur. There is no question that it's genocide and that there are horrible things going on in Darfur, but Sudan says 'No you can't come in' and certain members of the UN, the Security Council, say 'Yes we can't go in unless they ask us in'. How do we resolve this?

The US Foreign Policy Debate

The first reaction to the end of the Cold War was one of relief, relaxation and a certain amount of drift. There was no longer this existential threat that put you on edge all the time and made you think that you were going to do something which could precipitate a conflict. And thus we thought there was no need for strategic direction – which would have been a difficult task in any case given the dramatically changing world. So foreign policy became a little bit like donating to charity. It's a nice thing to do, but if you didn't want to it didn't make much difference. It was not that we were indifferent. It was just a lack of apparent threat and accompanying imperative to action. Then came 9/11, which was a profound shock to the United States because, unlike most of the world, enemy attacks don't happen in the United States. We haven't really had warfare in the United States since the Civil War.

There was Pearl Harbour, but that was 2,000 miles out in the Pacific. To have it happen at the heart of New York was a profound shock. It also awakened us to the fact that things were going on in the world which were really pretty serious, and we needed to focus on them.

The result of this was the stimulation of a philosophical division in attitudes towards US foreign policy already long present, but now in a new guise. For its first 100 years or so, the United States characterized itself principally as an example – the shining city on the hill, an example of man's ability (a certain amount of arrogance to this) to live in peace and harmony with his fellow men, which we learned from Britain and others but claimed as our own, of course. The philosophy was best enunciated by Washington and John Quincy Adams. The latter said:

> anywhere the flag of freedom and democracy is raised there will be our hearts, but we go not in search of monsters to destroy. We are the well-wishers of all who seek freedom but we are the guarantors only of our own.

That was our philosophy, and right after our war of independence the French Revolution started. The French emissary, Citizen Genais, came over and said, 'we helped you in your revolution, you help us', and we said, 'good luck'. In the Hungarian Revolution of 1848 the Hungarians raised a statue of liberty and cited the Declaration of Independence and came over and asked for help and we said, 'we wish you well'. That was our attitude until Woodrow Wilson; and Wilson said we need to be the evangelizers of democracy. It's not enough just to hold up the torch of freedom, we need to press it.

Since that time there has been a debate in American foreign policy – should we accept countries as they are, or should we try to change them? But after 9/11 this debate took on a new guise. I would call the current position – and these are my terms – the traditionalist versus the transformationalist. The traditionalists say we ought to go about our business in the world in company with our friends and our allies and international organizations. After all that is who we are. We are the ones who really were the driving force for NATO. We were the idea for the League of Nations. We were the idea for the UN. This is the way we do business. The transformationalists said no, the world is going bad and it's going bad very fast. We don't have time for this. We have all this power and while we have this power we need to use it to transform the world, and we can start that transformation by implanting democracy with the sword.

This transformational approach, though well-meaning, led us directly into Iraq, in order to use the great power that we had to begin the process of democratization in the most turbulent region of the world (and incidentally to demonstrate the awesomeness of US power so that no one would challenge us). Iraq has turned out, I think predictably, to be nothing like the transformationalists predicted. The stability in the Middle East, so decried by the transformationalists as stagnation, coddling dictators and so on, has indeed been ended, but it has been replaced by chaos rather than democracy. All the many separate problems of that difficult region – Afghanistan, Iran, Iraq, Palestine and terror – have been driven together and exacerbated. We, the United States, are now in a process of re-thinking our approach to this world and you can see it tentatively in many elements of US foreign policy. Unfortunately this process is now being caught up in an unusually extended election cycle, which tends to skew it.

How to Move Forward After Iraq

What are some of the principles on how we should move forward after Iraq? To me, first and primary is a reinvigoration of the Atlantic community. In this world of uncharted currents and uncertainty, it is critical that those of us who have a common view of man and his relationship to society and the state should band together. We have drifted apart both because of the disappearance of the glue of the Cold War and because of the friction engendered by the US and its new departures in foreign policy. It is time that we start to focus again on the problems of this world.

Among them is, for example, NATO. I have described how valuable NATO is, but what is it for? Can we turn it to good use for the world we now face? I think the answer is yes. But we are engaged in a critical struggle in Afghanistan and if we fail in Afghanistan, NATO is very likely not to survive in any meaningful form. Militarily we are doing reasonably well, but NATO is not fighting at its best. The various national troops have restrictions on their use which make it extremely difficult for the commander of the forces to use those troops in the most useful military ways. Overall in Afghanistan there is nobody in charge. The United States is in charge of the army, the Italians are in charge of the judiciary, the British are in charge of the police. But there's no one in charge of Afghanistan. Most of them report back to their own governments, not to somebody in Afghanistan who can say 'you don't do it that way, do it this way, and this has to be co-ordinated with that'. Thus we are at a critical juncture in NATO.

The United Nations is a natural haven in a globalized world, but it's a UN built for a different world – and I would suggest if we didn't have a UN at the moment we could not build one in the world today. We could not do what we did in 1945. The world is not in that kind of condition. So we need to take what we have and develop it to be useful. It's a very imperfect instrument. Secretary General Kofi Annan three years ago or so launched a major reform effort that largely failed. One of the chief perpetrators of that failure, I'm afraid, was the United States. We have had a very mixed view of the UN. It's been useful mostly because we can blame it for our own foreign policy mistakes. On the other hand there is a kind of irrational fear of some that it's about to take over the world and destroy the nation-state system. Kofi Annan submitted reforms to the General Assembly, and about three days before they were due to be debated the United States introduced 700 amendments. Need I say more?

We need to fix the UN. It badly needs reform. But there is an additional problem that has grown up, and that is the sense by the developing world that the UN (partly because of the structure of the Security Council and its permanent members) is dominated by the West. The developing world, by their numbers, control the General Assembly and therefore control the budget and control personnel. This problem is a major impediment to that kind of change. It is not beyond the will of all of us if we were carefully to make those changes, but we have a long way to go. The specialized agencies, the IMF and the World Bank, are sadly out of step. Neither the IMF nor the World Bank is doing anything remotely relating to the charters that they have. They need to be brought up to date. And the UN needs to resolve the contradiction between sovereign independence and the responsibility to protect – again, not an impossible job, but it will take careful, thoughtful strategy and diplomacy.

The Atlantic community needs a common strategy to encourage Russia toward the West. Russia is searching for its soul and that task could take a generation to settle down. The Russians need to decide how they want to govern themselves. We need to be patient and encouraging, and we need to end up with Russia as a member of the West. And we also need to act to encourage China to become, in the words of Bob Zoellick (the new chairman of the World Bank), a responsible stakeholder in the world. We have a good chance of doing that because China seems intent not on overturning the current world order but on profiting by it, and they are now heavily dependent on the world for raw materials, especially energy, and on markets for the goods they produce in such profusion. They have a stake in stability. To the extent that there is one, the West is the guarantor of stability. Lastly, I think we need to figure out how usefully to incorporate the Indias and the Brazils and the like into the world power structure.

We also must remember that, troubling as it is, this world does not face the mortal perils of the last century. If we behave wisely, prudently and in close strategic co-operation with each other, the twenty-first century could be the best yet in the rather dismal history of mankind.

8

THE UNITED STATES CANNOT STAND ALONE

Frank Carlucci

The immediate objectives of the Alliance have been pretty well spelled out by our leaders. Heading the priority list, of course, is limiting the proliferation of weapons of mass destruction and, above all, keeping them out of the hands of terrorists. Only with global co-operation can we achieve this goal. Given the nature of the threat, the time has come to think about ways we might eliminate them entirely, as Ronald Reagan wanted to do.

Another objective is reducing, possibly some day eliminating, the capacity of terrorists to do harm to our people and our way of life. We must find ways to dry up the sources of ongoing recruitment, much of which are in diaspora around the world. Once again international co-operation, particularly the sharing of intelligence, is critical.

Add to that related issues such as Iraq, the Peace Process and flashpoints like Taiwan, Korea, India and Pakistan and you have an enormous challenge for the Alliance, a challenge at least equal in complexity and severity to that of the Cold War.

Underlying many of these challenges are long-term issues – the unequal distribution of wealth around the world, and the growing gap between the West and Islam. Globalization complicates both these. The Alliance must join hands in finding a way to promote economic growth and a fair distribution of income in the most impoverished countries; if not, millions of people will become alienated from basic standards of civilization. Trade is key. We must resist the siren call of protectionism.

Understanding Different Cultures

There is no fundamental reason why the West and Islam cannot live together in peace, but radical groups are seeking to exploit Islam for their own purposes and the US, through some ill-considered statements and actions, has played into their hands. Some in Islam want to restore the Caliphate and many, if not most, Muslims believe the US is embarked on a new crusade in order to dominate the oil-rich Middle East. Democracy to them is a subtle effort to undermine Islam, since it entails separation of church and state.

We must deepen our understanding of each others' cultures and show greater sensitivity. Caution is an order on urging western concepts and practices on them. Along with this, we need to make a determined effort to promote the peace process. While we can and should be supportive of Israel, we should recognize that our interests are not identical with hers. It is not possible to be a partisan and a mediator at the same time.

And then there is China, which is destined to become a powerful force in the world. Managing that relationship will take all the skill the western powers can master.

Above all as we cope with these challenges, the US must recognize that, despite our power, we cannot alone shape the world to our liking. We can have a weighty influence on events but only if we regain our moral authority. Military might is not enough. We need co-operative relationships around the world today just as we did in the past. The Cold

War would never have ended when it did had it not been for NATO and the deployment of GLCMS and cruise missiles on European soil.

At the heart of the network that we need around the world to accomplish our objectives is the Western Alliance. And at the heart of that Alliance is a strong and enduring relationship between the United States and the United Kingdom. It is imperative that we keep it that way.

9

THE BRIDGE OF DREAMS

David Howell

The theory of the Blair years was excellent. The United Kingdom would be a bridge between a United States confident in its continuing task of leadership in the age of globalization and a Europe increasingly united, purposeful and dynamic.

This would put the British in – yes – a pivotal role, at the epicentre of world events, wonderfully positioned between Pax Americana and Pax Europa. Gone would be resigned or outright defeatist talk of the United Kingdom as the Athens to Washington's Rome, so widespread in the days of Harold Macmillan. And gone would be fears of the United Kingdom as the isolated offshore island of Europe, the other great terror of the Macmillan era, and one which still stalks the corridors of the Foreign Office in London to this day.

To work in practice this vision would require (i) that such a bridge was needed and would be used, (ii) that the United States remained firm and resolute in its global purposes, (iii) that Europe had a clear way forward as a cohesive and effective force on the world stage, and (iv) that the Atlantic alliance, linking the two continental entities (and their destinies) of the United States and the European Union, was still the dominant, agenda-setting partnership in global affairs.

Unfortunately, none of these conditions now apply. The bridge idea was perhaps fanciful from the start, a leftover vanity from history and World War II. What was much more reasonable to hope was that, despite fast-changing world conditions and new threats, and the terrible wound of 9/11, the United States would stay firmly and steadily at the head of the democracies, by far the wealthiest and mightiest nation in military terms, the natural leader with an experienced touch in turbulent times and dangerous new global conditions.

Surely this would be the safest assumption of all, that of all the nations on earth the United States would be the one that could and would adapt its outlook most swiftly and adroitly to the new global realities, and would understand most clearly where globalization was now taking everybody and everything. After all, didn't the Americans more or less invent the idea? And was not Wall Street the first to seize on its colossal financial implications, although London was nearly as quick off the mark? And have not a hundred Presidential utterances been peppered with references to the new global order (with the British Prime Minister, Tony Blair, the US's most trusted ally, doing his bit as well, especially after 9/11 with his vivid references to the kaleidoscope being shaken up and so on)?

Yet for all the flow of words from both leaders, it seems their heads were somewhere else. What they both missed is a central and fundamental point about this latest phase in human affairs – namely that what applies to money and what applies to communications also now applies to power. The amazing revolution in all things brought about by the information age, the internet, the explosion of consequent networking technologies and the combined chemistry of all this with global free markets has not only dispersed knowledge. It has dispersed and re-allocated power and influence on a scale never before known. It is not just a question of capitalism recruiting billions of new adherents in booming Asia. The power to command and control, the power to create and the power to destroy have all been lifted out of the hands of the old players.

The cards had been re-dealt, but the biggest players at the table seem fatally not to have noticed.

Nowhere on the surface are results of this apparent myopia more vivid and starker than in the Middle East imbroglio. In speech after speech President Bush and his colleagues have explained how the United States leads, how American strategy will reshape the region and how American military might (by many times the greatest defence arsenal in the world) must and will prevail. The US's allies, notably the United Kingdom, will help. But with or without friends, the US will overcome, the US will 'surge' – the latest misleading verb – and the US will succeed.

It is not just the White House and the administration who still see things this way. The abused neo-conservatives by no means have a monopoly of misunderstanding in this area. Even the President's harshest critics assume in their comments that the United States must lead the way out of the multiple crises that torture the Middle East (see for example the Iraq Study Group which, while critical of the Bush strategy, is steeped in the same assumptions about the US's central role). And for those who have doubts, there is the hostile world outside to prove their point, a gigantic echo-box of anti-American sentiment. Does not all the noise from outside confirm what Americans already know to be so – that they are the hegemon, the hyperpower, and that, like it or not, the world expects them to take centre stage and stay there?

The US Right on Energy

A twist to the tale of declining American influence or ability to shape world events has been provided by the world-wide climate debate. While European opinion, and that of many other countries, has become wedded to the idea of targets to make 'deep cuts' in the growth of carbon emissions, the USA, with one or two allies only, has stood out stubbornly against visionary targets and in favour of practical measures and maximum technological momentum in curbing greenhouse gases.

Weakened by its lost reputation in other fields the US administration has lost the public relations battle for common sense in climate issues and has been cornered in a welter of denunciations. Yet the supreme irony is that this stand may be one in which America is right and fashionable and excited opinion round the rest of the world is wrong. While all eyes are on targets the facts tell a different story. They show that the immense power of markets in combination with innovation and technological drive, in which America has excelled in the twentieth century, is delivering better results in reducing emissions than any amount of targeting.

The much vaunted European Emissions Trading Scheme has made many business operators rich but its impact on carbon emissions has been zero. The obsession with carbon footprints for everything, with dubious carbon offset schemes and with grandiose plans for the global administration of carbon measurement and pricing are taking half the world down blind and dangerous alleys. In better and different times America might be leading the globe along more realistic paths in these matters. But the tragedy is that the present voices who speak for the United States have lost their credibility and their power to command respect. Folly is proceeding in its onward march. And for this the world will pay a terrible price.

I would add that if current predictions as to the extent and speed of climate change are correct, and one must assume that they are, carbon reductions by the developed nations as proposed will only have a marginal influence, while of course in the newly industrialising world – China and India in particular – carbon emissions are likely to increase exponentially, dwarfing any savings that we might make. Apart from the American technological approach, the best way forward is to spend the vast sums already proposed on mitigating the impact of climate change – rather than Canute-like, seeking to stop it – for example through strengthened flood defences and the relocation of vulnerable populations away from low-lying coastal regions.

* * *

The US is unpopular – now almost universally – yes. But is this not the burden of world leadership? Has not a network of American-led alliances shaped the world since 1945, and who dares to say that the United States, with or without compliant allies in tow, should not carry on doing so as the 'respected leader' of nations? Well, the answers are now winging their way back and they are uncomfortable ones – so uncomfortable that it seems as though people just do not want to know.

What was obvious to some from the outset of the present era (although not, evidently, to now bewildered senior members of the Bush administration, nor to British Government leaders) was that democracy could not be delivered by overwhelming force; 'democracy' was too variegated and subtle a concept to be packaged up and sent overseas, and overwhelming force could no longer overwhelm.

What remains much less obvious up to this very moment is why, beneath the surface, the entire structure of assumptions about the US's power to control and influence world events has become flawed, in ways which were always bound to lead to the Iraqi fiasco and to strategic failure in the Middle East. This is what has yet to be grasped by those around George Bush, as well as his American opponents, and by those around the outgoing British Prime Minister. For them it remains unthinkable. Yet it is beginning to seep into the debate – the awful cold reality that turns the American dream into the American nightmare. And what is this reality? It is that the United States is no longer in charge, command or control. It is not in charge in Iraq, it was not in charge in the Lebanon in the summer of 2006. It is not even in charge in the Israel–Palestine conflict, where so many commentators keep calling for it to 'take a lead' or 'do something'.

But surely the United States is the biggest and the best, the boss nation, just as it has been since World War II? Alas, the world is no longer organized that way. There are no boss nations. Washington is not Rome because there is no Rome. And the United States is not at the centre of the world because there is no

centre, or not in the old power political sense. The whole structure of relationships between nations and forces has moved on,
from a vertical pattern of command and control – the big powers
calling the shots – to a network pattern of connections and co-
operation of infinitely greater subtlety and complexity.

In this new pattern, power has been miniaturized. The
microchip has put lethal force, as well as power for creative
good, into a thousand hands where one government or institution stood before. Ever more miniscule and yet more dangerous weapons have empowered groups far below the radar
screen of nation-states, rogue or otherwise, and levelled the
playing field of projected power in ways utterly baffling to traditional thinking.

On the one side are gigantic standing armies and arsenals
of missiles and nuclear warheads; on the other side are
e-enabled, e-coordinated terror teams, tiny groups with high-
tech weapons by their side, suicide squads, plotters stretching
out to get their hands on nuclear material, even single individual fanatics – all empowered and with the muscle to take
on giants, and to do so on terrifyingly equal terms. The age of
asymmetry has arrived with a vengeance.

These are deeply difficult and complex changes to compre-
hend. They overturn the mindsets of 50 years past, indeed of
the whole twentieth century. But until they are understood at
the top, it will not only be American influence, reputation and
foreign policy effectiveness which will remain hamstrung. It
will be the United Kingdom's position as well. This is where
the crucial changes have been missed, not just about the way
foreign policy should be conducted by great powers but about
the very latest phase in global affairs, which is quite unlike
anything that has gone before.

Does the possession of a still enormous stock of nuclear
weapons nonetheless give the United States the residual power
to dictate global strategy and guarantee national security? So
it might still be thought in Washington, despite the cruel
evidence of 9/11 to the contrary. The reality is that nuclear

warheads remain weapons of great danger but no longer weapons of power. The prospect of their potential further proliferation is indeed one of the age's most serious issues.

But nuclear warheads are weapons of deterrence between states, and to the extent that power has now drained away from states into other hands they are guarding the wrong gates. Furthermore there is no such thing as an independent nuclear capability. The entire system of nuclear weapons ownership is interdependent. The only conceivable way of fighting nuclear terrorism is by establishing new alliances of the most intimate collaborative kind between both the existing nuclear powers (including the United Kingdom, France and obviously Russia and China) and the other 'declared' nuclear states, India and Pakistan, a category into which Israel, too, has to be pressed.

The former five 'existing nuclear powers' are now enmeshed in a network in which every move down or up, that is whether to decommission or to upgrade, has to be taken in total co-operation with others. Neither the Washington debate on the US's role nor the poorly orchestrated debate in the UK on the upgrading of its Trident ballistic missile system seem to have taken any account of this new power distribution.

Asia the New Epicentre: Europe no Superpower

If the American delusion is that size and military weight still automatically mean global supremacy, a similar kind of delusion distorts Europe's progress. The high vision is of the EU as an emergent bloc or superpower, both partner to and counterweight against the American behemoth, and all part of the grand Atlantic world, the western world, the 'advanced' world.

In a staggeringly short space of time this has been invalidated and turned to dust. 'Asia is the epicentre of global politics and economics', declares Professor Chung Min Lee, one of the most respected authorities on East Asian security, as he opens his Trilateral Commission essay on the region, stating in a matter-of-fact way what he assumes all but the blindest now accept. The empires of the Atlantic world are no more. That phase of history is over.

Armies of statistics now support the Professor's assumption. In 2006 the JACIKS (Japan, ASEAN, China, India and Korea) accounted for 30% of the world's GNP, up from 24% three years earlier and about the same now as the EU. The region produces around 30% of the world's total exports. China now imports more than the United States, as its huge growth rate sucks up oil and raw materials on a swelling scale, as well as products for its fast expanding and already enormous consumer markets.

But this is not even half the story. The surging spread of free market capitalism has now brought, in the phrase of Clyde Prestowitz, 'three billion new capitalists' into the world system as power and opportunity have shifted eastwards. Of course, free markets were bound to spread anyway once the Communist bloc melted and the old free world solidarity against Communism, which tended to bury commercial differences and restrictions, dissolved with it. But it is the seamless opportunities of the website world which turn American-led capitalism into what Edward Luttwak christens turbo-capitalism and simply washes away the US's high ground, making it a level player in the flattened scene.

The process goes much further. The wildfire spread of capitalism throughout Asia, mixing with Confucian and other ethics of saving, have produced a gigantic financing system which now directly supports the deficit-ridden West, and the United States in particular. Vast Asian dollar reserves, and a readiness to keep holding them and indeed carry on accumulating them, now underpin US economic growth. Hitherto supposedly rock-solid European and American banking institutions turn to Asia for re-financing and support. China's trillion dollar reserves, plus Japan's $800 billion, plus Taiwan's and Hong Kong's hundreds of billions, and others besides, keeps the world's financial system in balance and in credit. Asia now literally holds the purse strings. And he who pays the piper ...

That American leaders should lecture their creditors on governance, democracy and political values, or assume blithely that their past leadership role remains unchanged, would be almost comical if it was not intensely dangerous.

Like it or not, power is shifting. It is shifting to Asia, where Japan, China and India are about to become the strategic drivers of world affairs, and it is shifting even more to individuals at their keyboards and to the colossal opportunities for collaboration and initiative that have fallen into their hands. Of course, extrapolations and trajectory forecasts can often be wrong-footed, it is true. When in the 1990s I described the coming rise of Asian power, not just in economic terms but in terms of superior moral and social cohesion, in a pamphlet entitled 'Easternisation', the subsequent hiccup caused by the Asian currency turmoil crisis was seized on by jeering critics (notably in *The Times*) to prove that this was all wrong.

It was wrong for about six months, before the far more powerful underlying trends, driven by the new ultra-accessible internet platforms, sent the fortunes and intentions of billions of motivated Asians soaring skywards again.

The same sort of chorus came on stage again with the collapse of the dotcom boom in 2000. Actually this event had the opposite effect, enabling multitudes of smaller enterprises to scoop up cheap communications infrastructures, such as fibre-optical networks, and to open new free platforms (so-called open sourcing) to unleash a torrent of new collaborative applications and procedures across the entire planet.

The effects went even further. Thanks to instantaneous interactivity on the web, and the google-ization of just about every activity and idea known to humankind, an entirely new pattern of supply chains has developed across the world. This is not just a matter of outsourcing chunks of production and processes from western bases to India and elsewhere. Nor is it just simply a matter of western business investors off-shoring their plants and assets into the new growth areas with lower labour costs.

What have now mushroomed in the last few years are supply chains of infinite complexity and with items and ideas flowing in both directions – to and from the new economies and feeding the swelling Chinese and Asian markets just as much as the western and Atlantic ones. Hundreds of millions of new middle-income Asian capitalists are now beginning to consume (as well as save) on a massive scale. Thus a single final product, whether a washing machine or an i-pod or something as complex as an airliner, can be drawing in components and knowledge inputs from umpteen western and Asian sources. National barriers and tariff walls are shrinking into insignificance and rearguard protective actions are now being fought through thinly disguised health and safety regulations (an EU speciality), desperately trying to catch up with the shuttle and swirl of transactions to and fro across the planet in every direction.

Self-organization and collaboration at every level of humanity decimate the power of governments and former unchallenged authorities – the governments of the Atlantic powers very much included, and the US very much included. Into individual hands the worldwide browser has tipped the power and capacity to create personalized worlds and intimate communities that are virtually independent of traditional social and official structures.

This is the context, super-global and super-local, in which elected nation-state leaders have now to carve out a continuing role. Down the ladder go notions of national or regional strategic supremacy, as no one is supreme in a network world. Down the ladder go impulses towards exclusive (ourselves alone) national security – all parts of the global network are vulnerable and an attack on any city or society is an attack on all. Down the ladder also go notions of national energy 'independence', an idea of breathtaking unrealism being much trumpeted by the Bush administration, demonstrating yet again a deep ignorance of the now totally integrated nature of global energy supplies. And down the ladder go conceits about national and unilateral economic management and protection. All national economies are now interwoven and totally interdependent.

By contrast, up the ladder come demands on national governments to be completely open and transparent, to deliver basic domestic services with infinitely greater efficiency and sensitivity, to respect local diversity and initiative far more readily, to ensure personal safety and security, and discourage lawlessness and crime much more comprehensively. On the geo-political front comes the priority mission to join ranks in coalitions and networks which minimize threats to national security and maximize the contribution which any nation can make to global peace and stability, thereby maximizing also any nation's sense of purpose, self-esteem and inner cohesion.

Few better explanations exist of why and how this enormous transformation in the geo-political realities has taken place than that offered by the wonderfully perceptive writer, Thomas Friedman, in his book *The World is Flat*, 2005. Friedman has arrived in a way that his countrymen high in the administration have not. Friedman now understands that for a whole range of reasons the globalization process, and the communications revolution driving it which the micro-chip set in motion some 25 years ago, has entered a third phase which changes everything.

This third phase is the one in which not only countries find themselves thrown into intimacy and interdependence on a scale never before imagined, as walls and barriers tumble, and not only companies and businesses everywhere find themselves drawn into entirely new global networks of services and supply chains. Thanks to the development of more and more internet-based applications and possibilities, the building of coalitions, projects and movements (good and bad) now falls into individual hands. Power becomes dispersed and flattened to an infinite degree, leaving central policy-planners, authorities and governments bereft of old instruments of authority and confronted by the need to adapt to completely new ones.

Actually, none of this is entirely new. Over a decade ago Manuel Castells was describing in immense detail how the 'informational revolution' would transform not only government but the whole structure of global relationships, in his three-volume publication *The Rise of the Network Society*, 1996. And to that some of us added our own warnings (for example, in my book *The Edge of Now – New Questions for Democracy in the Network Age*, 2000) that as power was dispersed, and as capitalism became totally globalized, as predicted quite accurately long ago by Karl Marx, western government ascendancy would pass to markets, to rising societies away from the Atlantic basin, as well as to malign and dangerous groupings in a near anarchic pattern.

The direct external implications for both Europe and for the United Kingdom of these fundamental re-alignments of power, of influence and of trends in human affairs, could not be clearer. We read that the German Chancellor, Angela Merkel, wants to see the EU's rapid further advance towards a bloc common foreign policy, that will have global impact towards a single constitution, and towards closer ties with the United States. Against the background described above, these three ambitions seem very wide of the target and rooted in yesterday's thinking, both for Germany and for the EU as a whole. No integrated regional bloc will hold together under the impact of the worldwide system of supply chain production and disintegrated power which the internet and the web have ushered into being.

If Germany or any other European nation wants security and protection of its civil society against terrorist attacks, and if it wants energy security and real and lasting benefits for its citizens, as well as a fully restored reputation as a responsible global player, it should be looking not only at greater European regional co-operation on local issues, which is always desirable, and not only at good relations with the United States, which are always worth having. More important now than either of those goals is the need to burnish relations with the rising powers and markets of Asia, where the key decisions will be made which will make or break worldwide terrorism, stabilize the Middle East and lift tens of millions out of poverty fastest.

Any European nation concerned about climate security, as we all are, should be looking to China and India for direct co-operation in fighting global warming, where decisions far more influential in cleaning the atmosphere than any carbon emissions trading scheme in Europe will have to be made. And any European nation wanting bigger markets should be looking at the already huge consumer power of South-East Asia, at Chinese markets and at internet markets. The mantra that the EU itself is the world's biggest market gets repeatedly asserted. It is no longer true.

If Germany wants more secure energy supplies it should look north to Norway, reduce its overdependence on Russia and resume nuclear power station building, with the latest and safest technologies, rather than put its faith in an EU common energy policy which will never happen.

The search should be on in every European nation for the new networks and linkages that will bring its citizens the most benefits in the new conditions. Time and energies spent trying to achieve unachievable ambitions for a united EU foreign policy and for a European state's place in the sun, or stretching for dreams of the EU as a new superpower, are far better spent reaching out and associating with the nodes of power in the new global network.

Amongst member states France has shown the most awareness of the new priorities – in Asia and elsewhere – whilst continuing with admirable dexterity to 'play' the EU scene and use the EU in ways best designed to assist France's aspirations (not least, to prevent the resurgence of an over-mighty Germany).

The New Role of the United Kingdom and the Commonwealth

But the most fortunately placed European nation of all is surely the UK, and this is certainly the almost universal view throughout the rest of the Union's membership as they look enviously at the UK's position. And what arouses this envy? Simply that the UK, like some lucky beneficiary of a large bequest, finds itself at the heart of a ready-made network which, given a little development, fits perfectly into the new global environment.

This network is the Commonwealth. Here is a quite extraordinarily latticed association of like-minded states, transcontinental, multifaith, embracing rich and poor, and which sits before the United Kingdom's eyes almost virtually on a plate (or more precisely with its headquarters and secretariat in the heart of London at Marlborough House).

Far from being a run-down club, held together by nostalgia and decolonization fixations, today's Commonwealth now contains 13 of the world's fastest growing economies, including the most potent emerging markets. Outside the United States and Japan, the key cutting-edge countries in information technology and e-commerce are all Commonwealth members. The new 'jewel in the Commonwealth Crown' turns out to be the old jewel, dramatically re-polished and re-set – namely booming India, the world's largest democracy with a population set to exceed China's.

By accident and luck, this is the kind of arrangement which is now almost perfectly tailored to fit into the new global scene, and offers both its members and the wider international community an ideal platform on which to work together in face of new threats and opportunities, as power both passes to Asia and is scattered across Thomas Friedman's flatter world.

Yet no official imagination has begun to focus on the possibilities and benefits. Not a single mention of the Commonwealth appeared in the most recent Report on the Work of the Foreign and Commonwealth Office – except in the unavoidable front page title! As for stronger interest in ASEAN, officials from Singapore and other dynamic Asian centres sigh and admit that they have failed to engage British interest in their region.

Building up the Commonwealth model depends, of course, upon all its leading member states. Until they wake up fully and understand the staggering potential of the new Commonwealth network as an ideal model for international collaboration in the twenty-first century, the backing needed will not be there. This means persuading Commonwealth governments to give place and recognition to the Commonwealth network in their foreign and overseas economic and development policies at a level which, for various reasons (mostly now outdated), they have hitherto failed to do. The big exception is India, which almost alone, with its new flair and dynamism, has recognized the Commonwealth as 'the ideal platform for business and trade'.

The failure in Washington thinking (as well as in London and Brussels circles) to understand what has happened, and the tragic collapse of the US's 'soft power', reputation and influence almost across the entire globe, is leaving a dangerous vacuum. Into this vacuum, cautiously, subtly but steadily are moving the Chinese – with cash, with investment projects, with trade deals and deals to secure access to oil and gas supplies in an energy hungry world, with military and policing support and with technology.

This is a gap which ought to be filled not by the Chinese dictatorship but by the free democracies of the Commonwealth, from both north and south, banded together by a commitment to freedom under the rule of law and ready to make real and common sacrifices in the interests of a peaceful and stable world and the spread of democratic governance in many different forms. The Commonwealth possesses the vital attributes for dealing with this new world, which the old twentieth-century institutions so conspicuously lack. It stretches across the faiths, with half a billion Muslim members; and it stretches across all the continents, thus by its very existence nullifying the dark analysis of a coming clash of civilizations.

Living by our wits on a small-ish, although still beautiful island and its appendages, in a subtly evolved union of kingdoms which has grown over centuries and which only the most shallow and short-sighted want to pull apart, we can least afford to stay tied to the tramlines of past thinking about the international order and the nature and distribution of global power, and we can least afford to pass up casually the huge advantages which by good fortune have come our way from past legacies.

Foreign Policy and the Power of Identity

Pollsters and focus group strategists tell us that 'foreign policy' is a low category in the list of people's concerns. Education, health, crime control and social policy come far ahead. But this is to misunderstand what foreign policy means. It is not just another category. It is the central question for every society and nation about its place and identity and purpose. There has to be a 'certain idea' of a nation, the way it should relate to other societies and the way it can best contribute to the larger common weal by which its own future stands or falls.

It is the primary duty of a nation's leaders to articulate and refine that idea. This task has now become ten times more important, as national security has to be re-defined, as the old power centres melt away, and as the control of so many parts of national life slips into remote hands or the anonymity of markets vastly empowered by the information revolution.

Never was it more important for a nation in the United Kingdom's position to seek out and work in the right and respectful relationship with the right new partners in the utterly transformed global conditions that have emerged and now prevail.

Our old partners, or so we thought, were across the Atlantic and next door in continental Europe. Our new partners are going to be in East Asia, in near and central Asia and in South-East Asia. These are the regions where tomorrow is being shaped, both economically and strategically. Indeed, our new partners are across the whole web-enabled, levelled planet.

10

FORGING NUCLEAR WARHEADS INTO LIGHTBULBS

Sam Nunn

On Veterans Day in 1948, at the dawn of the nuclear age after the devastation of Hiroshima and Nagasaki, General Omar Bradley said in a speech:

> The world has achieved brilliance without wisdom, power without conscience. Ours is a world of nuclear giants and ethical infants. We know more about war than we know about peace, more about killing than we know about living.

It might surprise General Bradley, if he were alive today, to know that we have made it 60 years without a nuclear catastrophe. Thousands of men and women thought deeply and worked diligently on both sides of the Iron Curtain to prevent nuclear war, to avoid overreacting to false warnings and to provide safety mechanisms and joint understanding to reduce risk. We were good, we were diligent, but we were also very lucky. We had more than a few close calls, including the Cuban Missile Crisis of 1962; the 1979 scare when a technician at Omaha accidentally loaded a simulated attack into our warning system; the 1983 Soviet warning glitch which falsely showed five nuclear missiles launched against it by the United States. India and Pakistan have already had more than one close call – and their nuclear age has just begun.

Making it through 60 years without a nuclear attack should not make us complacent. In the future, it won't be enough to be lucky once or twice. If we're to avoid a catastrophe, all nuclear powers still have to be highly capable, careful, competent, rational *and* lucky – every single time. We do have important preventive efforts underway and some successes, including the Nunn-Lugar Co-operative Threat Reduction program, the Global Threat Reduction Initiative, the Global Initiative to Combat Nuclear Terrorism, the Proliferation Security Initiative, the rollback of Libya's nuclear program and UN Resolution 1540.

These all mark progress and potential, but from my perspective the risk of a nuclear weapon being used today is growing, not receding. The storm clouds are gathering, and the situation can be summarized thus:

1. Terrorists are seeking nuclear weapons and there can be little doubt that if they acquire a weapon that they will use it.
2. There are nuclear weapons materials in more than 40 countries, some secured by nothing more than a chain link fence (wire netting). At the current pace, it will be several decades before this material is adequately secured or eliminated globally.
3. The know-how and expertise to build nuclear weapons is far more available today because of an explosion of information and commerce throughout the world.
4. The number of nuclear weapons states is increasing. Iran and North Korea's nuclear programs threaten to spark a nuclear arms race in the Middle East and Asia.
5. A world with 12 or 20 nuclear weapons states will be immeasurably more dangerous than today's world, and

make it more likely that weapons or materials to make them will fall into the hands of terrorists.

6. Our worst nightmare – the spread of nuclear capability to terrorist groups, with no return address and little way of being deterred – will become more likely.

7. With the growing interest in nuclear energy, a number of countries are considering developing the capacity to enrich uranium ostensibly to use as fuel for nuclear energy, but this would also give them the capacity to move quickly to a nuclear weapons program if they chose to do so. The *New York Times* recently reported that roughly a dozen states in the Middle East have recently turned to the International Atomic Energy Agency (IAEA) for help in starting their own nuclear programs.

8. The nuclear giants, the United States and Russia, continue to deploy thousands of nuclear weapons on ballistic missiles that can hit their targets in less than 30 minutes – with a short warning time and prompt launch capability that carries with it an increasingly unacceptable risk of an accidental, mistaken or unauthorized launch.

The bottom line is this – the accelerating spread of nuclear weapons, nuclear know-how and nuclear material has brought us to a nuclear tipping-point. The world is heading in a very dangerous direction.

The New Nuclear Threat

The greatest dangers of the Cold War were addressed primarily by *confrontation* with Moscow. The greatest threats we face today – catastrophic terrorism, a rise in the number of nuclear weapons states, increasing danger of mistaken, accidental or unauthorized nuclear launch – we can prevent only in *co-operation* with Moscow, Beijing and many other capitals. We must change direction. The good news is that I believe the security and economic interests of the great powers (the US,

Russia, China, Europe, Japan and India) have never been more aligned. As Henry Kissinger says, 'the great powers have nothing to gain by military conflict with each other. They are all dependent on the global economic system'. Old rivalries should not keep us from seeing common interests.

Both leaders and citizens of the US and abroad must reflect on what is at stake. If al-Qaida had hit the trade towers with a small crude nuclear weapon instead of two airplanes, a fireball would have vaporized everything in the vicinity. Lower Manhattan and the financial district would be ash and rubble. Tens of thousands of people would have been killed instantly. Those who survived would have been left with no shelter, no clean water, no safe food, no medical attention. Telecommunications, utilities, transportation and rescue services would have been thrown into chaos.

That would have been just the *physical* impact. If you were trying to draw a circle to mark the overall impact of the blast – in social, economic, and security terms – the circle would be the equator itself. No part of the planet would escape the impact. People everywhere would fear another blast. Travel, international trade, capital flows and commerce would virtually stop, and many freedoms we have come to take for granted would quickly be eroded in the name of security. The confidence of the United States and the world would be shaken to the core. From my perspective, we are in a race between co-operation and catastrophe.

With these growing dangers and stakes in mind, George Shultz, Bill Perry, Henry Kissinger and I published an op-ed (independent article) in the *Wall Street Journal* that called for a different direction for our global nuclear policy, with both vision and steps. We said that US leadership will be required to take the world to the next stage – to a solid consensus for reversing reliance on nuclear weapons globally. We see that as a vital contribution to preventing their proliferation into potentially dangerous hands and ultimately ending them as a threat to the world. We underscored the importance of intensive work with leaders of the countries in possession of nuclear weapons to turn the goal of a world without nuclear weapons into a joint enterprise. We made the point that terrorist groups are 'conceptually outside the bounds of a deterrent strategy', and even among states ('unless urgent new actions are taken') the US will find itself in a nuclear era 'more precarious, psychologically disorienting, and economically even more costly than was Cold War deterrence'.

The four of us and the many other former security leaders who joined us are keenly aware that the quest for a nuclear-free world is fraught with practical and political challenges. As the *Economist* magazine wisely said in 2006: 'By simply demanding the goal of a world without nuclear weapons, without a readiness to tackle the practical problems raised by it, ensures that it will never happen'. We have taken aim at the 'practical problems' by setting out a series of steps that we believe constitute the 'urgent new actions' for reducing the nuclear dangers, and lay the groundwork for building a world free of the nuclear threat.

The specific steps are as follows:

1. The United States and Russia should move to change the Cold War posture of their deployed nuclear weapons to increase greatly warning time in both countries and ease our fingers away from the nuclear trigger.
2. Nuclear forces should be reduced substantially in all states that possess them.
3. We must eliminate short-range 'tactical' nuclear weapons, the bombs most likely to be targeted for theft or purchase by terrorists, beginning with accountability and transparency between the United States and Russia.
4. We must work to bring the Comprehensive Test Ban Treaty into force, in the United States and in other key states.
5. We must secure nuclear weapons and materials around the world to the highest standards.

6. We must get control of the uranium enrichment process for civil nuclear fuel production, phase out the use of highly enriched uranium in civil commerce and halt the production of fissile material for weapons.

7. We must redouble efforts to resolve the regional confrontations that increase demand for nuclear weapons.

8. We must enhance our verification capabilities. President Reagan's credo 'trust, but verify' has been largely forgotten. We must make at least as much effort in building verification procedures and technology as we are now making in missile defence technology.

Each step will help reverse the spread of nuclear weapons. Each step is valuable not only for its ability to inspire greater co-operation, but for its own sake. Each step represents a move in the right direction. Each step reduces the risk of nuclear use.

No Security Without Co-operation and a Non-Nuclear Vision

None of these steps can be taken by the United States alone. Strategic co-operation must become the cornerstone of our national defense against nuclear weapons. This is not because co-operation gives us a warm feeling of community, but because every other method will fail.

I have concluded that we cannot defend the United States without taking these steps; we cannot take these steps without the co-operation of other nations; and we cannot get the co-operation of other nations without the vision and hope of a world that will some day end these weapons of mass destruction as a threat to that world.

The vision and action must go together. Without the bold vision, the actions will not be perceived as fair or urgent. Without the actions, the vision will not be perceived as realistic or possible. This cannot happen overnight. It will be a long process, done in stages. The United States must keep our nuclear weapons as long as other nations do. But we will be safer, and the world will be safer, if we are working toward the goal of de-emphasizing nuclear weapons and ultimately ridding our world of them.

The vision of a nuclear-free world is not new. In his memoirs, President Reagan wrote: 'For the eight years I was president, I never let my dream of a nuclear-free world fade from my mind'. In the 1960s, at an earlier tipping-point in the nuclear age, it was the vision of a nuclear-free world that pulled us back from the edge. It came in the form of the Nuclear Non-Proliferation Treaty. It was the grand bargain of the nuclear age, designed to limit the number of nuclear weapons states in the world. The Treaty was built on three promises:

1. The Article VI commitment of nuclear weapons states to move toward nuclear disarmament.
2. The commitment of non-nuclear weapons states to forego nuclear weapons.
3. The commitment that all nations should have access to nuclear technology for peaceful purposes.

This Treaty, and its vision of a world free of nuclear weapons, has been successful in keeping the number of nuclear weapons states below what almost anyone in the 1960s expected by the turn of the twentieth century. But today, the Treaty is in trouble. In the eyes of its critics, the Treaty has served to enshrine the nuclear weapons inequalities that existed the day it was signed. As they see it, those who had nuclear weapons on that day continue to keep them; those who didn't – tough luck. There can be endless argument about exactly what the Article VI commitment means and the timetable, but it must mean at least this: nuclear weapons nations must visibly and steadily reduce their reliance on nuclear weapons. Today the world believes they are not, and that belief has a clear and increasingly negative impact on our efforts to prevent the spread and use of nuclear weapons. As IAEA Director ElBaradei recently said: 'It's hard to tell people not to smoke when you have a cigarette dangling from your mouth'.

Recently, former Russian President Gorbachev endorsed the views expressed in our opinion piece, and stated:

> The members of the nuclear club should formally reiterate their commitment to reducing and ultimately eliminating nuclear weapons. As a token of their serious intent, they should without delay take two crucial steps – ratify the Comprehensive Test Ban Treaty and make changes in their military doctrines, removing nuclear weapons from the Cold War-era high alert status.

I believe the world should take up Gorbachev's challenge.

We should ask ourselves a long overdue question – 16 years after the Cold War, is it in the United States' national security interest for the President of Russia to have only a few minutes to decide whether to fire his nuclear weapons or lose them, in response to what could be a false warning? How can anyone think this is in our security interest? I would hope that this question would be asked in reverse in Russia and that we would begin to ask it together.

If both the United States and Russia altered their Cold War alert postures and significantly increased warning and decision time, we could dramatically reduce the chance of an accidental, mistaken or unauthorized launch. The benefits of working with Russia to remove our weapons from hair-trigger alert would have benefits beyond reducing the risk we pose one another. If we remove our nuclear missiles from hair-trigger – and at the same time reduce our numbers of nuclear weapons – it will strengthen our fight against the spread of nuclear weapons.

This is not because our example will inspire Iran, North Korea or al-Qaida to say 'we have seen the light', but because many more nations will be willing to join us in a firm and vigorous approach to stop the proliferation of nuclear weapons and materials and prevent catastrophic terrorism. The power of this kind of international pressure is crucial. If a strong coalition of nations bands together, it can exert powerful economic, diplomatic and military pressure to prevent new nuclear weapons states and make it much less likely that terrorists can get the materials they need to build a nuclear weapon.

The Mountain Top

The reaction of many people to the vision and steps to eliminate the nuclear threat comes in two parts. On the one hand they say, 'that would be great'. And their second thought is, 'We can never get there'. To me, the goal of a world free of nuclear weapons is like the top of a very tall mountain. It is tempting and easy to say that we can't get there from here. It is true that today in our troubled world we can't see the top of the mountain.

But we can see that at the moment we are heading down, rather than up. We can see that we must turn around, that we must take paths leading to higher ground and that we must get others to move with us. We can see that there are trails leading upward:

1. We can work with the Russians to remove weapons from hair-trigger alert and increase warning and decision time for both Russia and the United States.
2. We can work with other nations to reduce the number of nuclear weapons in the world.
3. We can work harder and faster to secure and eliminate nuclear weapons materials that could be bought or stolen by terrorists.
4. We can agree on transparency, accountability and near-term elimination of short-range battlefield nuclear weapons (a terrorist's dream).

5. We can greatly strengthen our verification capabilities.
6. We can redouble our efforts to ease regional confrontations that greatly increase the demand side of the nuclear equation.

Tough steps yes, but do-able. Once we get to higher ground there will remain serious obstacles between us and the top. We must develop ironclad verification procedures and assurances for monitoring and enforcing a prohibition on nuclear weapons. We must be able to respond quickly and decisively to any attempt to cheat. Today it is very apparent that our capability in this regard needs considerable strengthening. Both the good and bad news is that, given the big steps required to move upward, we have time to work on the transition from higher ground to the top. It is not too soon to begin.

Let me close with a parable of hope. After the collapse of the Soviet Union, when the United States began funding Russia's work to dismantle Soviet nuclear missiles and warheads, our countries struck a deal called the US–Russian Highly Enriched Uranium Agreement. Under this agreement, which was signed in 1993, 500 tons of highly enriched uranium from former Soviet nuclear weapons is being blended down to low enriched uranium, and then used as fuel for nuclear power plants in the United States. Shipments began in 1995 and will continue through 2013. When you calculate that 20% of all electricity in the US comes from nuclear power plants, and 50% of the nuclear fuel used in the US comes from Russia through the HEU Agreement, you have an interesting fact – roughly speaking, one out of every ten light bulbs in the United States today is powered by material that was in Soviet nuclear warheads pointed at us a few years ago. We have gone from swords to plowshares. Who would have thought this possible in the 1950s, 1960s, 1970s or 1980s? It would certainly have been seen as a mountain too high to climb.

Nearly 20 years ago President Reagan asked his audience to imagine we had discovered that we were threatened by a power from outer space, from another planet. The President then asked: 'Wouldn't we come together to fight that particular threat?' After letting that image sink in for a moment, President Reagan came to his point:

> We now have a weapon that can destroy the world. Why don't we recognize that threat more clearly and then come together with one aim in mind – how safely, sanely and quickly can we rid the world of this threat to our civilization and our existence.

If we want our children and grandchildren to ever see the mountain top, our generation must begin to answer this question.

11

THE CHALLENGE OF ENERGY SECURITY

Dick G. Lugar

In today's geo-strategic environment few threats are more perilous than the potential cut-off of energy supplies. The use of energy as a weapon is not a theoretical threat of the future; it is happening now. Energy is being used by those who possess it as leverage against their neighbours. In the years ahead the most likely source of armed conflict in the European theatre and the surrounding regions will be energy scarcity and manipulation. Overcoming US and European dependence on imported energy, and working together and with other nations to prevent energy crises, are fundamental national security imperatives on a par with controlling weapons of mass destruction.

We all hope that the economics of supply and pricing surrounding energy transactions will be rational and transparent. We hope that nations with abundant oil and natural gas will reliably supply these resources in normal market transactions to those who need them. We hope that pipelines, sea lanes and other means of transmission will be safe. We hope that energy cartels will not be formed to limit available supplies and manipulate markets. We hope that energy-rich nations will not exclude or confiscate productive foreign energy investments in the name of nationalism. And we hope that vast energy wealth will not be a source of corruption within nations that desperately ask their governments to develop and deliver the benefits of this wealth broadly to society.

Unfortunately, our experiences provide little reason to be confident that market rationality will be the governing force behind energy policy and transactions. The majority of oil and natural gas supplies and reserves in the world are not controlled by efficient, privately owned companies. Geology and politics have created oil and natural gas superpowers. According to one authoritative estimate, foreign governments control up to 79% of the world's oil reserves through their national oil companies. These governments set prices through their investment and production decisions, and they have wide latitude to shut off the taps for political reasons.

The vast majority of these oil assets are afflicted by at least one of three problems – lack of investment, political manipulation or the threat of instability and terrorism. As recently as 2002, spare production capacity exceeded world oil consumption by about 10%. As world demand for oil rapidly increased in the subsequent years, spare capacity has declined to 2% or less. Thus, even minor disruptions of oil supply can drive up prices. In 2006 a routine inspection found corrosion in a section of BP's Prudhoe Bay oil pipeline that shut down 8% of US oil output, causing a $2 spike in oil prices. That the oil market is this vulnerable to something as mundane as corrosion in a pipeline is evidence of the precarious conditions in which we live.

Because natural gas is traded regionally, and because Europe is dependent on a few suppliers, the risk that natural gas supplies will be used as political leverage against an individual country is even greater than for oil.

Less widely acknowledged are the ways in which energy constrains our foreign policy options, limiting effectiveness in some cases and forcing our hand in others. We pressure Sudan to stop genocide in Darfur, but we find that the Sudanese government is insulated by oil revenue and oil supply relationships. We try to persuade Iran to stop its uranium enrichment activities, yet key nations are hesitant to endanger their access to Iran's oil and natural gas. We try to foster global respect for civil society and human rights, yet oil revenues flowing to authoritarian governments are often diverted to corrupt or repressive purposes. We fight terrorism, yet some of the hundreds of billions of dollars we spend each year on energy imports is diverted to terrorists. We give foreign assistance to lift people out of poverty, yet energy-poor countries are further impoverished by expensive energy import bills. We seek options that would allow for military disengagement in Iraq and the wider Middle East, yet our way of life depends on a steady stream of oil from that region.

Ending the West's oil import dependence will not suddenly cure poverty, end terrorism, prevent weapons proliferation or bring peace to the Middle East. But failing to address oil dependence guarantees that our pursuit of these foreign policy goals will be encumbered and our way of life will remain under threat. European and American national security will be at risk as long as we are heavily dependent on imported energy.

The Need for US Leadership

As the world's largest consumer of imported energy, the United States has a special obligation to lead. Yet while Americans and their leaders are embracing the idea of changing our energy destiny, we have not committed ourselves to the action steps required to achieve an alternative future. In fact, advancements in American energy security have been painfully slow, and political leadership has been defensive, rather than pro-active. One can point with appreciation to a few positive trends, but in the context of our larger energy vulnerability, progress has not been sufficient. If our economy is crippled by an oil embargo, if terrorists succeed in disrupting our oil lifeline, or if we slide into a war because oil wealth has emboldened hostile regimes, it will not matter that before disaster struck the American public and its leaders gained a new sense of realism about our vulnerability. It will not matter that we were producing marginally more ethanol than before or that consumers are more willing to consider hybrids and other alternative vehicles. Achieving a positive trend line is almost inevitable as long as energy costs remain high, because these costs will lead to some improvements in investment and conservation. We need to have the discipline to understand that a modestly positive trend line is not enough.

Breaking through a political logjam often requires a crisis that focuses the nation in a way that achieves a consensus. But consider that the combination of September 11, 2001, the war in Iraq, the conflict on the Israeli-Lebanese border, the nuclear stand-offs with Iran and North Korea, Russia's temporary natural gas cut-offs to Europe, the Katrina and Rita hurricanes and several other severe problems did not create a consensus on energy policy. The American people are angered by $3.00 gasoline, but they still buy it in record quantities. This leads one to the sobering conclusion that a disaster capable of sufficiently energizing public opinion and our political structures will have to be something worse than the collective maladies listed above – perhaps extreme enough to push the price of oil to triple digits and set in motion a worldwide economic downturn. None of us want to experience this or any of the other nightmare scenarios that await us. It is time to summon the political will to overcome the energy stalemate.

President Bush and whoever succeeds him must be willing to commit the prestige of their administrations to overcoming American energy deficiencies. They must be capable of absorbing political and technological setbacks along the way, without bending on the necessity of achieving the chosen goals. Congress and private enterprise can make evolutionary energy advancements, but revolutionary national progress in the energy field probably is dependent on presidential action. Our energy dependence is perpetuated by a lack of national will and focus. We must elevate the cause to national status, and leverage the buying power, regulatory authority and legislative leadership of the entire government behind solving a problem that is highly conducive to political procrastination.

Prospects for success would be enhanced if the goals were well-publicized, measurable and understandable to the broad public. In the best case, such goals would take on a symbolic identity that transcends dry provisions in energy bills or statements in a State of the Union speech. In the best case, progress toward these goals would stimulate a degree of American pride.

Although there is no shortage of potential energy goals to choose from, I would highlight two such goals to illustrate the concept. Firstly, President Bush or his successor could establish the national goal of making competitively priced biofuels available to every motorist in the United States. Such an accomplishment would transform our transportation sector and cut dramatically our oil dependency. Such a campaign could achieve the replacement of 6.5 million barrels of oil per day by volume – the rough equivalent of one third of the oil used in the United States and one half of our current oil imports.

Secondly, the President could commit to increasing radically the gasoline and diesel mileage of the US's auto fleet. Given that other developed nations have made great strides in improving fuel economy, this is fertile ground for rapid improvement. In fact, achievements on this front largely would be a matter of generating and sustaining political will that has, thus far, been absent. Incredibly, cars in the United States today get less mileage per gallon than they did 20 years ago. Meanwhile hybrids, plug-in hybrids and fully electric cars are at or nearly at commercialization.

The Role of NATO and the EU

A strong American commitment to reduce sharply our own import dependence is a necessary ingredient to enhancing the West's security, but it is not sufficient. We must take bold steps co-operatively as well. It would be irresponsible for the European Union and NATO to decline involvement in energy security, when it is apparent that the jobs, health and security of our modern economies and societies depend on the sufficiency and timely availability of diverse energy resources. Energy may seem to be a less lethal weapon than military force, but a sustained natural gas shutdown to a European country in the middle of winter could cause death and economic loss on the scale of a military attack. Moreover, in such circumstances nations would become desperate, increasing the chances of armed conflict and terrorism.

The transatlantic community must move now to address our energy vulnerability. Sufficient investment and planning cannot happen overnight, and it will take years to change behaviour, construct successful strategies and build supporting infrastructure. No issue is more likely to divide allies in the absence of concerted action.

In 2006 I delivered a speech at a conference prior to the start of the NATO summit in Riga, Latvia. I urged leaders to identify the response to an energy cut-off as an Article V commitment and develop an action plan to respond to such events. Article V of the NATO Charter classifies an attack on one member as an attack on all. Originally envisioned to respond to an armed invasion, this commitment was the bedrock of our Cold War alliance and a powerful symbol of unity that deterred aggression for nearly 50 years. It was also designed to prevent coercion of a NATO member by a non-member state.

I am not suggesting that the Atlantic Alliance respond to energy cut-offs with military force. Rather, I am advocating that the Alliance commit itself to preparing a range of options for jointly deterring the use of energy as a weapon and responding if such an event occurs. Though at that time I focused on NATO's role, I would applaud greater preparation and co-ordination on energy by the EU as well. Although attention to energy security issues is expanding within NATO and the EU, neither has so far demonstrated the decisiveness and cohesion that are required.

The transatlantic community must develop a strategy that includes the re-supply of a victim of an aggressive energy suspension. Alternatives to existing pipeline routes must be identified, and financial and political support for the development of alternative energy sources is crucial to deterring the use of energy as a weapon. A co-ordinated and well-publicized transatlantic response would reduce the chances of miscalculation or military conflict. This will not be easy or comfortable. States will be required to tighten their belts and make hard choices. But, if we fail to prepare, we will intensify our predicament.

Perhaps the most important short-term energy mission of the Alliance is to provide diplomatic and economic support for alternative energy routes from Central Asia and the Caucasus. Diversity of energy supply and transportation would be strengthened with Caspian oil and gas, yet necessary interconnections to bring the fuels directly to Europe are stalled. The political and diplomatic difficulty of establishing such connections was demonstrated most recently in May 2007, when Turkmenistan elected to sign a new deal to send gas to Europe through Kazakhstan and Russia, rather than through a proposed pipeline under the Caspian to Azerbaijan and Turkey (a route that would be far preferable in terms of diversity of supply). Meanwhile, individual European countries are tempted to reach bilateral deals with energy suppliers. The impetus to do so is understandable. But these bilateral deals must not prevent unified action. Each of our political and economic bargaining positions is strengthened when we act in concert.

The Atlantic Alliance also should co-operate in expanding the global strategic petroleum reserve co-ordinating system.

Global reserves are co-ordinated through the International Energy Agency. Membership in the current system is limited and should be expanded to include major consuming nations, such as India and China. Given that oil is a globally traded commodity, a strategic reserve system that lacks participation by major consuming nations will never be as effective as it should be. In addition Alliance countries should expand their own oil reserves, and ensure that they are at least meeting treaty obligations to maintain prescribed levels of petroleum products.

A greater challenge is creating a co-ordinating system for natural gas in case of emergency supply shortages. Such a system would require the resolution of many political and technical questions regarding how reserve natural gas would be stored, transported and shared. It would likely require additional infrastructure to transfer alternative gas supplies. We would also have to plan for rapid transitions to alternative power sources where practicable. But the value of a natural gas emergency co-ordinating mechanism in preventing or responding to a crisis could be incalculable.

As we strive for Alliance unity in meeting these challenges, the United States and Europe must narrow the gaps between our national energy priorities. Europeans have demonstrated more political will than Americans in dealing with climate change, while Americans have been more concerned with geo-political factors in the international energy debate. I am optimistic that transatlantic views are converging. There is an increasing recognition, for example, that we must rapidly deploy alternative energy and energy efficiency technologies, and that successful deployment will be enhanced by international co-operative endeavours.

In 2007 I wrote to German Chancellor Angela Merkel, urging her government to focus on energy security during Germany's presidency of the European Union. At the May 2007 US-EU summit in Washington, the two sides gave unprecedented attention to energy security issues, calling for international co-operation on increasing energy efficiency, diversifying energy supplies (including the share of renewable energies) and protecting and maintaining the world's energy supply system. The communiqué contained a work action plan that can serve as a useful starting point for intensified transatlantic co-operation going forward.

Beyond constructing strong policies related to energy, a united transatlantic community must engage Russia and other energy rich nations. We must speak clearly with Russia and other energy producers about our concerns and our determination to protect our economies and our peoples. We should ensure that competition, transparency and antitrust rules form the basis of international energy transactions – an objective endorsed at the St Petersburg G8 summit. In the best case, Russia would comply with the Energy Charter Treaty of 1994 and the Transit Protocol. More broadly we should outline the clear benefits of a future in which Russia solidifies consumer-producer trust with the West, and respects energy investments that help expand and maintain production capacity. The fickleness of energy markets affects not only consumers, but producers. Energy is a two-way relationship, and will remain so even as Europe and the United States diversify their energy resource base.

By their nature, alliances require constant study and revision if they are to be resilient and relevant. They must examine the needs of their members and determine how the freedom, prosperity and security of each member can be safeguarded. For more than a half century the transatlantic community has prospered while meeting common threats and expanding the zone of peace and security across Europe. But if we fail to reorient the transatlantic relationship to address energy security, we will be ignoring the dynamic that is most likely to spur conflict and threaten the well-being of alliance members.

If the transatlantic community stands together, we have significant leverage. If we are divided, then one EU or NATO member can be played off against another. Policy experts can find consensus on what should be done, but it is up to politicians and national leaders to summon the will and public support to act decisively, and soon. The stakes are such that if we wait even a few years, we are likely to find our security in further jeopardy.

12

WHO WILL *DO* FOREIGN POLICY?

John Coles

A question for the next British government – you will decide what objectives you want to pursue in foreign policy, but have you the instruments to do it? If you need to send troops to fight abroad, then they are surely entitled to the best expertise we can offer on the area of operation. If you want to prevent conflict, combat terrorism, crime and drugs, and stem proliferation of weapons of mass destruction, you will need people with serious working experience of the countries that are the source of these problems. As the effects of climate change gather pace, there will be unprecedented strains on individual countries and the international system as a whole. Again professional experience of abroad will be at a premium. But the capacity of the Foreign Office to provide such expertise has long been in decline, and is now a serious problem.

Shortly after I retired as Permanent Under-Secretary at the Foreign Office in 1997, I wrote a book *(Making Foreign Policy. A Certain Idea of Britain,* 2000) which discussed the strengths and weaknesses of foreign policy in the United Kingdom. A good deal has changed. I commented on the lack of strategic planning. In 2003 Jack Straw published for the first time an 'international strategy', and promised to update it every two years. I advocated an Annual White Paper on foreign policy, for which ministers in my time showed no enthusiasm. In March 2006 Jack Straw presented to Parliament 'Active Diplomacy for a Changing World', setting out for the government as a whole, not just the Foreign Office, international strategic priorities for the future.

The Foreign Office itself has changed markedly since I left it. But the problem of declining capacity to provide the government with expert analysis of, and advice about, countries and regions remains. This was one of my biggest concerns as Permanent Under-Secretary and it is widely shared by former British diplomats who have watched the decline over the last two or three decades. They and I are not looking back to some golden age. There wasn't one. But we can all recall a past time when the quality of Foreign Office expertise on key countries and regions of the world was much stronger than it is now. Wherever in the world a crisis or serious issue arose, the government usually had to hand diplomats of stature and authority whose advice and judgement were based on long and deep experience of the area in question. It was what the Foreign Office did best.

Diplomats are not the only people who have noted the decline. The services provided by the Foreign Office to British business have in general improved significantly. But it is relatively common to find leading companies who have searched in vain for the regional expertise that was so valuable to them in the past, and who have concluded that their own staff are now better informed about their areas of operation than the Foreign Office.

If there is an inquiry into the decision to intervene militarily in Iraq, and if, as I hope, it examines the lessons to be learned, then it should certainly consider what knowledge and experience of that country was available to the government, whether expert advice was listened to and whether it was passed to the United States government and with what result.

From the outside it seemed that the Foreign Office had considerable difficulty in finding people with the requisite experience to advise on the problem and to staff the various missions in Iraq. And it has not been hard to detect a feeling that such expert advice as was available was not properly sought.

The intelligence failures in Iraq have been exhaustively examined and debated. But a decision to commit to military intervention can never be based solely or even largely on intelligence. The more important considerations are the objectives you hope to achieve, your plans to achieve them, your assessment of the likely impact on the country concerned and your longer-term view of what rebuilding activity will be needed when the fighting is over. Judgements on all these matters need to be based on local and regional realities, on the expertise of those who know the region from practical experience of working in it. It is not the role of the intelligence agencies to offer judgements of this sort.

The Need for Expertise

The precise nature of the expertise required obviously varies from country to country. But as a rough guide embassies (not just ambassadors) need to have good working relationships with key decision-makers and opinion-formers, and to have ready access to government ministers, opposition politicians, security authorities, heads of financial and other economic institutions and leading figures in the business sector and civil society. They need to understand the real as opposed to the formal decision-making processes, to track political, economic, social and cultural trends, to be alert to sources of dissent and protest and to influence opinion widely in the country. Capacity for political, economic and social analysis, strong interpersonal and communication skills and, often, good knowledge of local languages are needed.

The expertise accumulated by embassies has a strong practical quality because it stems from the daily business of working in local conditions to get things done, to achieve British objectives, to persuade key people and institutions to pursue policies or take action which help British policy. That experience in turn gives the advice and judgements conveyed by the embassy to London a tested and practical quality that journalists, academics, think-tanks and others cannot be expected to have because their trades are different.

It is obvious that the kind of expertise I have described can only be built up over time. A diplomat new to the area will need to be well into his or her posting before the process is anything like under way. To be effective, embassies need at least some people who have worked in the country, or at least the region, before. Similar considerations apply to the staffing of departments in London. That entails long-term planning and commitment.

The expertise needed in missions to international institutions, as distinct from embassies, is to some extent different in kind, but where these organizations are dealing with regional issues (as is usually the case with, for example, the UN Security Council) the diplomacy of the British mission needs to be informed by expertise from the field, from the country or region under discussion. Another distinct category of expertise has long been valuable in British diplomacy and needs to be sustained. The Foreign Office calls it 'functional', meaning that it is more related to issues than to geographical areas, for example arms control, defence, counter-terrorism and human rights.

There is no point in having experts unless their advice is sought and listened to. There may well be political or other factors that dictate that it cannot always be followed, but a government that decides not to follow expert advice should be clear that it has good reasons for its decision. A government that gives the impression that it does not want to hear the advice of experts is making a strong contribution to the decline of expertise.

That decline has probably been exacerbated by the now familiar domination of the Prime Minister and his office in foreign policy. When I worked in that office (1981 to 1984) its function was largely to ensure that the right expert advice was available to the Prime Minister at the right time. In the last 20 years its status and staff have expanded, and it has tended to become an alternative source of advice and an independent source of action on foreign policy. That almost certainly means that the quality of advice reaching the Prime Minister is inferior.

I am *not* arguing that present British diplomats are less capable than their predecessors. The quality of new recruits was consistently high during my period of service and I believe it remains so. The problems lie elsewhere. Fundamentally, demands on the Foreign Office in the shape of new tasks and new priorities have multiplied, resources have not increased commensurately and there have therefore been fewer available for the core functions of analysis and diplomacy.

New Tasks for the Foreign Office

In the 2006 White Paper mentioned above, Jack Straw writes:

> British people rely on the active diplomacy of the
> Foreign and Commonwealth Office to ensure that their
> interests are protected overseas. The most visible way
> the FCO does this is through its public services.

He cites examples from a 12-month period, including responding to hurricanes in the US and Mexico and to terrorist bombings in Egypt, dealing with some 3.5 million enquiries, issuing nearly half a million passports (and many more visas) and providing support to around 84,000 British people in distress. To which he adds support of British business and work to attract inward investment. Twenty years ago an account of the department's activities would have given nothing like so much prominence to these functions, except perhaps to that of supporting British firms. The world has changed. All these functions are necessary today. But if increased resources are devoted to them, and if the cake remains about the same size, then there is less for other things. The White Paper tells us that about one third of Foreign Office staff are now delivering services to British business, to those thinking of visiting or investing in the United Kingdom and to UK citizens.

Like other government departments, the Foreign Office is obliged to try to deliver the 'Professional Skills for Government Core Competence Target'. This process is 'designed to ensure that civil servants have the skills and experience needed to deliver good public services'. But what about the non-public services – the provision of analysis and advice, and the conduct of negotiations, much of it unpublicized, on the big issues of peace and war, terrorism, crime and so much else which in the end have much greater capacity to affect the lives of British citizens? And in any event public services (for example, travel advice, evacuation plans, responses to emergencies of one type and another, help for citizens in trouble abroad and assistance for firms) are unlikely to be of high quality unless they are grounded in experience and understanding of local conditions.

There is a danger that the concentration of resources and attention on public services will weaken what should be the principal activity of the Foreign Office, namely the efficient and successful delivery of the objectives of the government in foreign policy through negotiation and action, both in international organizations and in individual countries. This prime task requires both expert knowledge of organizations, regions and countries, and expertise in negotiation itself.

The White Paper sets out nine strategic international priorities for the government as a whole, which can be summarized as follows:

1. Dealing with global terrorism and weapons of mass destruction.

2. Combating international crime.
3. Preventing and resolving conflict.
4. Building an effective and globally competitive EU.
5. Supporting the economy and business.
6. Promoting sustainable development and poverty reduction.
7. Managing migration.
8. Supporting British nationals abroad.
9. Ensuring the security and good governance of the UK's overseas territories.

It is hard to imagine that a future government would abandon any of these priorities, though the list would be improved by adding the task of promoting action to minimize the adverse effects of climate change as a strategic priority in its own right. (It appears in the White Paper merely as one of the aspects of promoting sustainable development.) In the case of each of these priorities, achievement will be limited unless the work is informed by regional realities.

An annexe to the Paper sets out specific aims for the Foreign Office in working towards the priorities. The aims are too numerous to discuss here, but it is doubtful whether any of them can be pursued with any hope of success unless there is a strong injection of regional expertise. For example, in dealing with global terrorism the Foreign Office sets itself the task 'in partnership with Muslim governments, leaders, scholars and others' to 'counter the ideological and theological underpinnings of the terrorists' arguments and help prevent radicalization and terrorist recruitment, particularly among the young, in the UK and overseas'. If I were running an embassy with that task in a medium-sized Arab country, I would need on my staff a group of Arabic speakers with considerable experience of working in the Middle East and high-quality interpersonal and communication skills. And they would have many other tasks as well.

As a further example, in the strategic objective of preventing and resolving conflict the department is allocated the job of ensuring 'effective international action to tackle conflict, in particular in Iraq, Afghanistan, the Balkans and Eastern Europe, the Middle East, Sudan and elsewhere in Africa and South Asia'. This is quite an agenda! To be sure, this activity is to be pursued by working with other departments, especially the Ministry of Defence and the Department for International Development. But if the Foreign Office is not in a position to provide the necessary analysis of local conditions and issues in all these countries, no other department can fill the gap.

Unless the governments of the world are much more successful that I expect them to be in taking action soon enough to avoid the worst effects of global warming, then we are in for a future of unprecedented strains on the international system – natural disasters ranging from drought to flooding, very large movements of refugees, the breakdown of political and economic systems. The network of British diplomatic posts should be invaluable in tracking the practical impact of climate change on individual countries and advocating sensible precautionary and preventive measures. But they would need to be properly equipped and staffed for the task.

Overstretched Embassies

British governments have said, for as long as I can remember, that they wish the country's foreign policy to be *global*. By which they did not mean, at least in the last two decades, that they saw the United Kingdom as a global *power* but rather as a country with interests and influence spread across the globe that they wished to preserve and protect. So a worldwide network of diplomatic posts has been maintained (262 in 2006, which looks an impressive number). But over half have only four or less UK-based staff, and some are run entirely by staff engaged in the country in question and who are typically citizens of that country.

The cloth is stretched very thin. To see how thin, you have to examine particular posts. I have space for only one example – Central Asia. British business, especially the oil and gas industry, has invested billions of pounds in Central Asia. The 2006 Diplomatic List shows that in Kazakhstan there were nine diplomatic staff. Subtract those engaged in management, consular, British Council and commercial work and you are left with possibly four who might be engaged in political analysis and diplomatic activity, though I would guess that not more than one or two spend the bulk of their time in this way. In Kyrgystan there were no resident British staff. The work is done from Kazakhstan by virtually the same people who deal with the latter country. In Tajikistan there were four resident staff, in Uzbekistan nine (of whom perhaps three carry out the core political and diplomatic functions), with a similar number in Turkmenistan. The list does not reveal how many have the linguistic and other skills that the core tasks require. To my knowledge, some British firms have pressed for years for stronger diplomatic representation in Central Asia but without much success.

People cost money, and if there is not enough in the budget then the people cannot be provided. In 2005/6 the Foreign Office budget was £1.8 billion, but £790 million of this was earmarked for the BBC World Service, the British council and subscriptions to international organizations, and was thus not available for core functions. The core budget was about £1 billion (0.2% of public spending as a whole), not greatly more than when I left the Foreign Office in 1997. Meanwhile, expenditure on the UK's overseas aid programme leapt to nearly £4.5 billion in 2006.

The budget comes under particular strain when a major development in the world requires a new deployment of staff. Such was the case when the Soviet Union collapsed and embassies were required in a number of new independent states. Today there is a process of redeployment to India, China and elsewhere in Asia in recognition of their substantial and growing economic and political importance. But with an inadequate budget these shifts can only be achieved by

stripping posts in other regions of staff. Bodies can be transferred but how many of them will bring with them experience
and knowledge of their new destinations? It takes many years
to build up the expertise that makes a diplomat credible to the
host government and opinion-formers more widely. And
there is always the danger that some of the countries in which
it is judged safe to reduce the diplomatic staff will turn out to
be unexpectedly important, perhaps even vital to the pursuit
of the strategic priorities in the White Paper. Who knows
today which of them will become new sources of terrorism,
crime or conflict, or even new areas of interest to British firms?

The Task for the Next Government

Much foreign policy is highly rhetorical. Speeches, statements
and media interviews rarely reach more than a small audience, and are quickly forgotten even by them. A government
that wants more than rhetoric, that wants a serious effort to
achieve objectives abroad needs to look closely at how it is
going to do that. The Foreign Office is only one of the available
instruments but it, uniquely, has a presence across the globe.
Action is needed, not to recreate some mythical Diplomatic
Service of the past but to build one fit for purpose today and in
the future. The next British government should state that it
intends to make the Foreign Office and its overseas posts the
best possible source of country and regional expertise to
inform the whole range of foreign policy activity. It should
direct that a plan be prepared to achieve that aim and sustain
it in the years ahead, showing what staff will be required
where, what skills they will need, what training they will
receive. The plan should be fully costed, but it can be safely
said in advance that the total extra expenditure will be a small
fraction of the increase in the budget of DFID over the last few
years.

This needs to be a long-term investment. The expertise discussed here inevitably takes a long time to build up. It is an

investment that any responsible government should make. Without it, the chances of events harming British citizens will increase markedly. One of the lessons of the recent experience in Iraq, Afghanistan and to some extent the Balkans, is that there are strict limits on what the western alliance, or some of it, can expect to achieve by the use of force. We shall need to use diplomatic skills more and more to protect our interests. And for that we need diplomats, in sufficient numbers, who have not just the interpersonal and communications skills that the job demands but the deep, practical experience of living and working abroad that gives them analysis, advice and judgement, a reality that no other source can provide.

13

NATIONAL SECURITY IN THE AGE OF TERRORISM

Chas W. Freeman, Jr.

This is not a happy time for national security policy. There is the strategic ambush of Iraq to manage before it explodes into a wider war. North Korea is trying again to get our attention, and this time it has missiles and the bomb with which to do so, although progress has recently been made on this issue. Iran is well along in replacing the US as the dominant influence in the Middle East, and is widely believed to be working on a nuclear deterrent to the air raids on it by Israel or the US that leaders there and here are threatening. Hamas, which has never run an operation against Americans, and Hezbollah, which hasn't done so for decades, seem to be psyching themselves up to respond in kind to our violent efforts to crush them. The Taliban are making a comeback in Afghanistan, which just brought in the largest poppy harvest in history. The Venezuelans are replacing the Cubans as our adversaries in this hemisphere and, unlike the Cubans, they've got oil and money to buy allies for their endeavour. China is rising and the dollar is declining. We have never been so politically estranged from or so much in debt to foreigners. Our only committed ally in Europe, Tony Blair, has just left office. And this is just a partial list of the problems threatening the general welfare, domestic tranquillity and liberties of Americans.

There's nothing new, of course, about the world being a troublesome place. Four decades ago Secretary of State Dean Rusk said: 'At any moment of the day or night, two-thirds of the world's people are awake, and some of them are up to no good'. What is new, as 9/11 showed, is that there is no longer anything much to stop our enemies from coming after us in our homeland. Foreign policy is therefore no longer some nasty thing that Americans do to foreigners; it is also something that they can do back to us, sometimes with fatal results. It's not just that foreign policy has become more important to our national well-being and personal peace of mind.

What we do at home also has a much bigger bearing than before, not only on our domestic tranquillity, but on the support we can expect from the rest of the world. What we do at home is now a major factor in determining who's with us and who's against us beyond our borders. Increasingly, as all the polls show, people abroad are against us. Many of our former friends believe we have repudiated the values we once stood for. Our country has far fewer admirers overseas than it used to. But we do, manifestly, have a growing number of enemies. That's not the sort of trade-off we should welcome. And the post-Cold War world in which it is taking place is a great deal less ordered and predictable than the bipolar order that preceded it.

It is not that the dangers we face are greater. They are not. In the Cold War, the turn of a key in Moscow could have brought death to 60m Americans within minutes or hours and to another 80m or so within days or weeks. Horrible as a repetition of 9/11 or even a weapon of mass destruction in an American city would be, we no longer face a threat to our national existence comparable to the one we endured from 1939 to 1989. It will, on reflection, strike any veteran of the Cold War as ironic that, with so much less to be frightened about, we seem so much more fearful than before. But no one can deny that the threats we now face are real. And no politician dares to put them in perspective. In the earlier and simpler era of the Cold War, the Soviet Union was truly determined both to do us in and to conquer the world, but its leaders tried very hard to prevent its client states and captive political movements from attacking us. They did not want to be dragged into a nuclear exchange in which all but a few Russians and most Americans would die.

But the USSR is gone. No overlord has taken Moscow's place as the leader of those with a reason to hate us. The foreign enemies we make no longer have a patron; they're on their own. So, if we kill foreigners in their homelands, there's no one they care about with a stake in stopping them from trying to kill us in ours. We must do this thankless task ourselves. We must do it by dissolving their motivation to assault us, draining them of their resolve, dissuading them from the path of violence, deterring those who cannot be dissuaded and killing those who cannot be deterred. This is the formula the British applied to their long struggle with the various elements of the IRA. It is the approach that Saudi Arabia has more recently applied with equal success to the suppression of terrorist opposition to the Saudi monarchy.

Athens, not Sparta

Our approach requires a sophisticated strategy that supports conservative values against radical assault by discrediting extremist ideology. It demands effective diplomatic and political outreach, backed by sound economic and social policies. It asks of us that we understand our enemies and act to divide rather than unite them. It depends on sophisticated intelligence collection, analysis and law enforcement, backed as needed by the military in ways that do not make more enemies than they eliminate. And it rests on the recognition that we cannot preserve or defend our values and freedoms effectively by setting them aside or curtailing them and becoming more like our enemies than our former selves. We must remain Athens, not Sparta.

The problems we confront in Iraq and on other less central fronts in our confrontation with anti-American terrorists are primarily political, not military. What we lack is not military might but political acumen. Our failings are not those of muscle but of the mind. The US's principal policy co-ordination mechanisms were created in 1947, when Congress overrode President Truman's objections and mandated the formation of a National Security Council. The NSC system worked fine in the Cold War, which is what it was set up to deal with. But judging purely by results, it has not been able to co-ordinate responses to the more complex politico-military problems we now confront.

Our current policy co-ordination system failed to produce a war termination strategy during its first post-Cold War challenge, when we liberated Kuwait from Saddam's occupation; that war never really ended. Our national command authority failed to set achievable goals and stick to them in Somalia. It was for long ineffectual in coping with Bosnia. It fumbled our response to the open emergence of a nuclear arms race between India and Pakistan. It did not focus our leadership on the challenge of terrorists with global reach until they had actually attacked us. It has defaulted on the search for peace between Israelis, Palestinians and other Arabs. It has proven unable to set clear objectives or produce a strategy for achieving them in Afghanistan. It has yet to produce anything resembling a coherent strategy for dealing with North Korea or Iran or, for that matter, China or Russia or the European Union or the United Nations. It has not even tried to address our growing reliance on imports of foreign energy and money to sustain our lifestyle or the effects on our country of the mounting crisis in the global environment.

Clearly, with the State and Defence departments much of the time not even on speaking terms, it bungled the policy co-ordination role in Iraq and continues to do so. There seems to be a pattern emerging. It is not reducible to convenient partisan dimensions. This pattern of incompetence has cost us our international following. To lead a team you must know how to be a team player. To inspire people or nations to follow you, a reputation for moral uprightness, wisdom and veracity is essential. To retain authority you must demonstrate the capacity to reward as well as to punish, and you have to rack up a record of success. To sustain the loyalty of your followers you must be loyal to them, and considerate of their views and interests as well as your own. To hold other people or nations to rules you must show that you are prepared to follow them too.

We all know these things. Why don't we act accordingly? Part of the reason is that Americans perceive that we are no longer seen as exemplifying the characteristics of leadership, cited above, as we traditionally did. A large majority of citizens believe that the way we now deal with national security issues has made the United States (as well as the rest of the world) less, rather than more, safe. Nearly eight in ten respondents in one recent survey thought the world saw the US as 'arrogant', and nearly 90% said such negative perceptions threaten national security. They're right to be concerned.

The Military-Industrial Complex

The reaction to the next major terrorist attack on the United States will not resemble the outpouring of sympathy and support that followed 9/11. Our recovery from our strategic debacle in the Middle East will not be as rapid or sure as our recovery from defeat in Vietnam. There's no common enemy, no Soviet Union, to compel our allies and friends to stick with us. It would be comforting but wrong to blame most of these problems on the executive branch. The Congress bears considerable responsibility as well. Not only has it largely defaulted on its foreign policy oversight role in recent years, but its resistance to the reorganization of committee jurisdictions has made it impossible even to study how to reorganize the executive branch, let alone to do it. It would, I think, make sense for the Congress and the executive branch to begin this year jointly to consider how to enable the government to develop the more sophisticated policy co-ordination that today's more complex problems demand.

The way we put things together now does not always make sense. Let me cite the example of our spending on military and related functions. We put much more effort into national defence and security than most people realize. In fiscal 2006, our defence budget was $441.5 billion. This was a good bit more than the combined military spending of the world's other 192 countries. It amounted to 3.6% or so of our economy – which is, by a wide margin, still the largest on the planet. But, huge as it is, the defence budget is only part of what we spend on past, present and future wars. When we estimate military expenditures in countries like China, we quite appropriately include a lot of defence-related expenditures that are outside the official defence budget. If we were to apply the same standard to figuring out our own military spending, we would have to add to our defence budget the supplementals to pay for the wars in Afghanistan and Iraq, the nuclear weapons and naval propulsion systems in the Department of Energy budget, veterans programmes in the Veteran Association budget, military pensions funded by the Treasury, homeland security programmes, various intelligence activities and so forth. And we would find that, even without including interest on the money we borrow to fund it, our total national defence effort comes in at around $720 billion, or about 5.7% of GDP.

It's worth asking too whether scattering national security-related expenditures all over the federal budget in such a way that no one can tell you how much we spend on them is the best way to avoid redundancy and get the biggest bang for the buck. At any rate, all this spending has given us what are without doubt the most competent and lethal armed forces in history, and that's a very commendable result. But, as President Eisenhower foretold, we have also built a truly enormous and very influential military-industrial complex. Defence contractors interact incredibly effectively with Congress. One new and instructive example is that in the summer of 2003, the newly established Department of Homeland Security drew up a list of 160 sites in our country that terrorists might see as targets. Intense efforts to gain access to this new source of federal funding immediately led to the widening of the definition of potential targets. Within a few months, there were 1,849 targets. By the end of 2004, there were 28,360. Today bearded terrorists in the remote caves of Waziristan are officially feared to be planning attacks on about 300,000 targets all over the US, including, I was truly shocked and awed to learn, the Indiana Apple and Pork Festival. (I'm sure they lose a lot of sleep in Waziristan over that one.) Evidently, our system is extraordinarily good at funding military and related functions as well as at finding ways to spread money around, but one is left to wonder whether it is optimally designed to cope with the challenges to our security and domestic tranquillity in the twenty-first century.

The Al Capone Approach

Clearly, too, our political culture is good at enacting sanctions – and launching wars when sanctions fail, as they inevitably do – but is it competent at dealing with the challenges we now face? These aren't trivial questions. Why do we Americans think we should suspend common sense when we deal with foreigners? Why do we imagine that our differences with foreign miscreants require techniques of influence we would never apply to people here? What is it in our experience that causes us to suppose that trying to put them out of business, pulling a gun on them, beating them up or blowing up part of their property will cause them to repent and be saved, to mend their evil ways, and to embrace truth, justice and the

American way? Do we really think that public insults and a refusal to meet or talk with people with whom we disagree are the best way to persuade them to embrace our viewpoint? Do we truly believe that politely explaining to foreign leaders that what they are doing is both wrong and not in their interest is a sign of weakness? Would we reason the same way about Americans with whom we disagree? Do we judge that ostracism and beatings are the best way to teach even dogs and children to behave, let alone hostile adults? If not, why do we allow those who appear to believe these absurd things bully those who don't into silence?

Al Capone, who was as American as the Colt revolver, once remarked that, 'you will get more with a kind word and a gun than with a kind word alone'. True enough, but why omit the kind word? And do we want to be seen as the heirs of Al Capone in our approach to the world? Of course, talking is better than not talking only if you know what you're trying to accomplish and what you're going to say. And there's a reason that the use of force is generally regarded as a last resort; if you use it up front and it fails, diplomacy can't do much to rectify the facts you've created on the ground.

So we are back to the need to formulate strategies, set objectives and stick to them. We're going to need that capacity more than ever over the years to come. Here are a few items that pretty clearly need tending. The first three are so obvious that I'm almost embarrassed to mention them. First is the Middle East. As the Baker-Hamilton Iraq Study Group pointed out, there's more to the Middle East than just Iraq and the region needs to be addressed as a whole. In Iraq, the options are all bad and not improving. They seem to boil down to 'talk and walk', as recommended by the Study Group; 'cut and run', as many might prefer; or 'surge and scourge', as the neo-conservatives are trying to persuade the Decider to decide, despite much military advice to the contrary. Who knows whether anything at all can work at this point? What's clear is that our occupation is in deepening difficulty. The conflict in

Iraq is in real danger of triggering a wider war even as it continues to spawn a new generation of anti-American terrorists. There is mounting reason for concern about an assault on the 'green zone' modelled, perhaps, on the Tet Offensive in Vietnam.

Meanwhile, Iran continues to gain regional influence and to work at bomb-building; there's still no peace process; Israel is back at settlement-building and trying to bomb Palestinians into peaceful co-existence with it; no Arab leader wants a photo op with us; Lebanon has been ravaged and destabilized; the Turks and Kurds are eyeing each other with mounting belligerence; there are all sorts of rumours of covert action programmes directed at regime change in Syria and plans to bomb whatever nuclear-related targets we can find in Iran; and the Saudis and other Gulf Arabs are for the first time openly denouncing US policy. If that's not an explosive mixture, I don't know what is. It is certainly the stuff of which terrorism is born.

Next is Afghanistan. We have made the country safe for the poppy cultivators and warlords, but not for democracy. A well-focused effort to capture the perpetrators of 9/11, punish their hosts and deter others from hosting them has deteriorated into an aimless effort at pacification. This has endowed the Taliban with nationalist credentials they do not deserve. Meanwhile, in the broader Islamic world, Afghanistan is now seen as evidence of a broad American-led assault by the West on all Muslims. No one can say what victory in Afghanistan would look like for us. This is an unfolding tragedy that needs a rethink.

Finally, there is North Korea. Anyone who's had a kid that went through the 'terrible twos' will have no difficulty recognizing Kim Jong-Il's effort to gain attention for what it is. Outsourcing diplomacy to China isn't an effective response to this. We are now in the lull before the next tantrum, which will likely be pretty provocative – even unnerving – and involve missiles, shooting incidents or further nuclear blasts.

The Economic Dimension

Let me briefly mention three other issues of concern, each of which illustrates the interconnectedness of domestic and foreign affairs.

Firstly there is the problem of the US dollar. Every day, we must persuade foreigners to lend us more than $2 billion so that we can keep our government in business, our interest rates low and our employment rate high. So far we've been able to talk them into this. But, as someone famously once said, if something can't go on forever, sooner or later it will end. Foreign willingness to lend money to us at advantageous interest rates could end at any time.

If we let things get to the point where foreign lenders pull the plug on us, we will face interest charges at levels not seen since the 1970s. The housing and stock markets will implode, the price of everything from oil to laptops will skyrocket and there will be a sharp rise in unemployment. In addition to badly screwing up our domestic economy and politics, a dollar collapse would displace us from the centre of the global economy and catalyse a major, highly unfavourable shift in the balance of power. It's the sort of national security development that is worth trying hard to prevent. To do so, we need to get our act back together at home.

Second is the problem of US complacency. Americans are used to embodying superlatives; being the biggest and the best at almost everything. But it's hard to be proud that we are recognized abroad as the world's largest debtor, its biggest market for illegal narcotics, its most prolific producer of pornography and its most profligate consumer of imported energy. Concerned foreigners also know that we have the world's highest divorce rate, the biggest proportion of our adult population in prison and the most elevated rate of infant mortality in the developed world. And they see that we're not necessarily the best anymore in every field. The WHO ranks our health care system 37th in the world in overall quality, on a par with

Cuba. Graduates of our high schools believe they are in the 90th percentile internationally, but are actually in the 10th.

I could cite other examples but that would be too depressing. So I'll just reiterate the obvious. We have a lot of issues to deal with at home as well as abroad. As a result of the growing gap between our smug self-image and the way people overseas perceive us, we're neither as attractive to the rest of the world nor as sought after as we once were. This shows up clearly in polling data, but an additional measure of it is that, despite the fall in the dollar, fewer highly educated and wealthy foreigners want to come here. There is a diminished foreign student presence here even as the foreign student population in Europe, Japan, China, Australia, New Zealand and Canada is growing dramatically. There's a lot of anecdotal evidence to suggest that we are no longer attracting the very best. Meanwhile, our share of the global tourism market has fallen from 9% at the turn of the century to less than 6% today. Complacency is the enemy of excellence. We appear to have a bad case of it. We need to recover from it.

Thirdly, we need to address American competitiveness. Only 15% of our college students graduate in science and technology. In China, the figure is 50%. Traditionally, we've made up our shortage of brains by importing them. The geek may yet inherit the Earth, but post-9/11 they won't do it from here because they can't get visas to do it. As a result, our graduate schools are now short of teaching assistants and our labs are short of engineers. Our companies are responding by moving their Research and Development and other high tech operations to China and India. In part for this reason, New York has fallen to number three, behind Hong Kong and London, in the number of IPOs by new companies. These are microcosms of a much larger issue. Our exceptional openness to ideas and to people was what enabled us to lead the global advance of science and technology and to build an unprecedentedly innovative society. Now we are much less welcoming. If we don't do something about this trend, we are in danger of losing our economic leadership, as well as our political leadership of the world. That need not be; we must not let it come to pass.

We all grew up in a US that acknowledged its flaws, but that was justly admired and respected internationally. Our country then led with the force of its example rather than by the power of its armed forces. I lament the unnecessary passing of that appealingly introspective US. I suppose that brands me too as passé; I admit to being a geezer. But I remain hopeful that I will once again be part of a nation made attractive by its principles, wise by its experience, shrewd by its realism and prudent by its modesty. Such a country, proficient at arms and the arts of persuasion alike, would again have the world's support, not its animosity. Such a country could hope to manage successfully the challenges of national security in the age of terrorism. The United States can be born again.

14

THE NEW 'GREAT POWER' POLITICS

Michael Howard

The words 'British Foreign Policy' still have a grandiose Palmerstonian ring about them. They suggest an activity carried on by dignified ambassadors, chosen from an elite elevated far above officials concerned with mundane questions of domestic, financial and commercial affairs, discussing with their equally distinguished foreign colleagues such fundamental issues as alliances, the initiation and conclusion of war and the establishment and preservation of peace. But if it was ever like this, it is so no longer. Our relations with the rest of the world are no longer a matter of uni-dimensional contacts between the representatives of sovereign states. Embassies are now often little more than hotels whose rooms are filled by a transient population of experts on such questions as finance, trade, intelligence, policing, immigration, aid, oil, agriculture, transport and the environment, to name but a few; experts who have come to confer with others of their kind and report back to their own superiors in Whitehall or Brussels, about whose activities His or Her Excellency may or may not be kept fully informed but over which they have little if any control. Foreign policy is now a whole bundle of activities conducted at every conceivable level. In this globally interpenetrating age it is quite inseparable from domestic policy. Events in Pakistan or Baghdad can have serious if not sinister repercussions in Toxteth or Leicester, and vice-versa.

Furthermore, the United Kingdom is no longer an independent actor on the world stage; or rather, there are very few issues on which her independent action can have any effect. Palmerston may have been right when he said that the United Kingdom had no permanent friends or permanent enemies, but if we wish to affect events beyond our own shores we badly need partners. To secure and retain partners two requisites are necessary. First, we must have shared interests with them, and second we must ourselves be, in the German expression, *bundnisfahig* – that is, worth having as an ally.

These two requisites are in fact symbiotic. The primary, if not the sole, object of our foreign policy must be the security and prosperity of the population of these islands, whose standard of living depends on global trade. That in itself posits a peaceful global environment, one not threatened by disruptive social upheaval or cultural enmities that may erupt into major conflicts and, whether they directly threaten us or not, threaten the stability of an increasingly interdependent global community. In short we need peace; for only peace will enable us to be sufficiently prosperous and secure, politically, economically and militarily, to be worth having as a partner at all.

Throughout the 'short' twentieth century, from 1914 till 1989, the question of partners largely settled itself. There was a clear adversary, first Germany and then the Soviet Union, whose policies threatened the world order on which our own security and prosperity depended. That adversary could be neutralized only in partnership, first with our European neighbours, but ultimately with the United States. Our dependence on American good will, if not active partnership, was already clear by 1916 and had become desperately obvious in 1940, and remained so throughout the Cold War. As for Europe, after 1945 our interest lay first in restoring its prosperity and protecting its territory to make it an effective military ally, and then to help convert what had for centuries been a cockpit of conflict into a major political entity that would be a major factor for global stability.

Within both these partnerships, now melded into a single 'Western Alliance', there were inevitable frictions that kept our diplomats busy, but the perception of a common threat and the existence of multiple common interests ensured that the underlying framework remained unshaken. The main object of British foreign policy was to preserve this framework, but also to ensure that confrontation with the Soviet Union did not overbalance into catastrophic nuclear war. As for the rest of the world, where our former empire had left us both influence and interests, our main concern (after a nasty wobble over Suez in 1956) was to ensure that post-colonial resentment did not alienate our former possessions, and to help them develop economies that would ensure their wealth and stability and strengthen our own.

The end of the Cold War at first did nothing to change this situation. The Western Alliance not only survived, but was enlarged. Our former adversaries showed themselves almost pathetically anxious to join us by creating market economies, and the Russian example was followed by all her former satellites, with the exception only of Cuba and North Korea. The First Gulf War only cemented the alliance, especially our own partnership with the United States. The conflicts in the former Yugoslavia tested it but found it secure. In the Middle East, where our interests came closest to diverging from that of the United States, the Clinton administration presided over the nearest approach to an Israeli–Palestinian détente that the region had yet seen. Even the shock of 9/11 did not shake the alliance. Not only its members but its former adversaries joined immediately and unanimously in sympathy with the United States, and in support for its action against Afghanistan.

But 9/11 revealed a new factor in international relations – the existence throughout much of the world of a deep and widespread reaction against the dominance, not simply of western political and economic power, but of western ideology as a whole. This reaction found its deepest roots in certain small extremist Muslim sects, but inspired a global conspiracy, inconsiderable in numbers but made dangerous by its readiness to use extreme measures of terrorization, by its appeal to the disaffected throughout the Muslim diaspora, and by a simmering resentment throughout the Arab world of American power and influence (a resentment stoked by American support for an Israel whose suppression of Palestinian independence had embittered three generations).

Some alarmed analysts saw the need for a total 'paradigm shift'. They saw the world as no longer divided vertically between culturally diverse and ideologically motivated nation-states, but divided horizontally. On the one hand was a global community whose members might have diverse political systems, but shared a common interest in global stability and economic development. On the other was a transnational movement, at present lacking any serious state base (rather like the communist movement before 1917), and concerned rather with undermining the stability of an order it perceived as evil and alien rather than creating any serious alternative. In this last respect it differed from the comparable threats to international order that had been posed by liberal nationalism after 1815 or communism in the twentieth century, but like them it presented a challenge both to domestic and to international stability.

This was the analysis that guided the United States administration when it decided, in spite of international disagreement and domestic protest, not only to attack al-Qaida's bases in Afghanistan but to break ranks with its former allies and invade Iraq. Their action was guided by the belief that the United States was now 'at war' on a global scale with an elusive but ubiquitous adversary – a war that she had the strength, and if necessary the duty, to wage unilaterally. American military power, they maintained, could and should be used anywhere in the world to eliminate threats to American interests, to cow her adversaries and to establish regional stability, especially throughout the Middle East. Whether Saddam Hussein was directly linked with al-Qaida or not, they argued that his elimination was a necessary move in the waging of a 'global war against terror'.

This view was not widely shared by the rest of the world, and American action stretched the western alliance to breaking point. The British government allowed a visceral loyalty to 'the special relationship' to override the doubts expressed by its expert advisers, and joined in the invasion of Iraq. The result was a disaster. The invasion certainly succeeded in eliminating a hideous regime, but it shattered the alliance, exacerbated anti-western sentiments throughout the world, deepened the fault-lines in multiracial societies and encouraged global terrorism.

Repairing our Partnership with the United States

In the aftermath of this disaster, what should British foreign policy be?

Firstly our partnership with the United States should not be abandoned, but repaired. Whatever her faults, the United States remains an indispensable partner. We may have been wrong to associate ourselves so closely with a policy flawed in execution if not in concept, but it would certainly be wrong to dissociate ourselves now. Indeed, as her close associate, we have a particular responsibility to help her extricate herself from what is now generally admitted to have been a terrible error, something that the Bush administration and any likely successor is only too anxious to do. Our influence over American policy may be slight, but our support over Iraq made a deep impression on American public opinion and could be effective in guiding it back to the path of multilateralism – and to a realization that not even the United States can function effectively in the world without partners.

Certainly we should not align ourselves with any kind of anti-American European bloc. We should continue to work in Europe for close relations with the United States, and we should no more abdicate control of our policy to Brussels than we should to Washington. But to maintain a proper relationship with both we need a clear vision of our own interests in a very much more complex world than that of the last century. We are no longer confronting a totalitarian threat. Nor, menacing though it may seem, does global terrorism take its place as an existential threat to the international system. It is certainly a new and very ugly element in international relations, but it is not the only one, nor indeed the most important.

In some respects indeed we are seeing the emergence of a new kind of 'great power' politics, in which the actors are the United States, a loose European federation, a reviving and resentful Russia, China and India emerging as members of the club and a malevolent Iran, skilfully playing all against one another. But in addition there is a deeply troubled Islamic world stretching from the Mediterranean to the Far East, with a volatile diaspora in European cities and Palestine at its centre as a festering sore. There is an Africa rich in raw materials coveted by developing economies, but where natural disasters and ethnic hatreds defy attempts to establish peaceful order. All these elements are linked by a global dependence on oil, and the prospect of an apparently inexorable climatic transformation threatening mass migration and bitter conflicts over natural resources.

To deal with the most basic of these threats, we need not only the partnership of our traditional allies but the co-operation of a global community acting through such bodies as the G8 and the United Nations. That in its turn assumes governments who share our perspectives on the dangers that threaten the world and our approach to their solution. They are more likely to do this if they share our interest in their own economic and social development, which will make them more interested in peaceful co-operation than national or ethnic aggrandizement. This does not mean that they are necessarily 'democratic', but that their rulers can preserve an effective and consensual order, encouraging the development of an educated population and a thriving entrepreneurial and professional middle class whose interests are linked with that of the global community as a whole.

A vital element of our foreign policy should therefore be to encourage this development and provide the expertise to assist it – technological, medical, administrative, educational; all the experts, in fact, to whom our hapless ambassadors find themselves playing host. For this, our experience with the Commonwealth gives us an advantage shared by few other developed countries. The 'C' in FCO is a heritage to be exploited rather than an embarrassment best ignored. But if this contribution is to be effective, we have to be capable of producing these experts, and to maintain institutes of higher education in this country to which the rest of the world find it worth their while to send their young elites. That is an aspect of educational policy in this country that seldom receives the attention it deserves.

Finally, among these experts will be the military. One of the most useful functions now served by our armed forces, especially the army, is training and support for their opposite numbers in friendly developing countries. But that is not their primary function. They exist to fight. Traditionally the primary characteristic of *bundnisfahigkeit* has always been the capacity to provide an army that makes one a valuable ally or a formidable foe. That has certainly been the case with the British armed forces for the past 100 years. Efficient and available armed forces are a vital tool of foreign policy, even though it should be that policy to ensure that if possible they do not have to be used. The performance of British forces in the Falklands campaign gave them, and their country, a prestige unequalled anywhere in the world. That in Iraq has been greeted with respect, tempered by doubt as to whether they should be there at all.

But military prestige is an expendable asset. We have armed forces capable of fighting far from their home base very effectively, but not for very long. For sustained effort they are dependent, as indeed they were in the Falklands, on American support. Must we accept this as a necessary condition of military effectiveness? Or do we try, at great expense, to create an alternative military structure with our European allies? Or do we trust that small and efficient forces with limited range and capability, backed by a nuclear capacity, will be enough to ensure our military security in a diverse and dangerous world?

Even to pose these choices reveals that we have no alternative but the first. Our alliance with the United States is a matter of harsh political necessity, especially since we may during the coming century have to confront very much more dangerous adversaries than al-Qaida. But we must not let that necessity be blurred by sentiment. American interests are not identical with our own, and her perception of world problems is often widely different. But when we do differ in our analysis, there will be many Americans who will do the same, and our voice will not be alone in that splendidly disputatious and still free country. If we withhold our support for what we judge to be a mistaken initiative, as we did over Vietnam, we will have plenty of friends in Washington who will thank us for doing so. By asserting our independence of judgement we are as likely to increase the respect in which we are held as an ally as to diminish it. Certainly we should never again allow ourselves to get into the position of appearing to fight someone else's wars.

15

DEMOCRACY IN THE MIDDLE EAST

Mark Allen

The anecdote bears repeating of the US Secretary of State's farewell meetings with new American ambassadors before they set off for their missions. He would casually ask them, as he showed them out, 'Just show me on this globe, Mr Ambassador, exactly where your country is'. Most, of course, pointed to their destinations and not to the United States. They got savaged.

The ambassadors' mistake was only a silly slip, but the Secretary of State was gunning for an attitude he wanted to stamp out – a craven attitude to the local source of power. 'Postitis', 'localitis' and 'clientitis' are jargon expressions for the condition, thought to be endemic among ambassadors, of arguing the locals' case rather than staying in line with the government at home. Foreign affairs provide plenty of scope for grand street theatre, stereotypes and caricatures and Punch and Judy cameos of pretension and humiliation, and that is why the Secretary of State's story is retold and enjoyed. It tells us that things are as bad as we thought. We roll our eyes and the tragi-comedy rolls on.

In the background, beyond easy view, perhaps other influences are at work. Not the least of these is subtle fashion, the collective likes and dislikes of those in power at home. This mood takes an à la carte view of the foreign scene and insists on choosing, being subjective and positive. It knows that commentators and specialists in international affairs distinguish various schools – realist, ethical, pragmatic or 'values-based' – and it wants one of its own, a characterization which will set a new tone. The intention is not necessarily improper and may even be presented as a policy, a platform. But there is a hazard. Likes and dislikes make poor friends when trying to work out what is going on in the world and what may be done about it. Likes and dislikes may mistake what is incidental for what is fundamental and miscalculate what may be 'unacceptable' when, in fact, we have no choice but to accept it.

So the caricature ambassador is familiar to us, but there is also injustice in the parody that is often simply a prejudice, a resistance to the effort of understanding what is strange or unwelcome. And this is a prejudice of considerable strength. It makes very much more difficult the hard task the ambassador already faces. For the ambassador needs to communicate to his government at home how matters stand in the country or region where he is serving. He needs to explain the character and behaviour of power, and these will likely be thickly veiled by cultural considerations which are unfamiliar to us. It is hard to understand from the other side of the street and so the ambassador has to cross and walk into the crowd, to gauge its temper and its fears and aspirations. To achieve this without loss of judgement, without the head being turned by the admiring or minatory attentions of the local power centre and without losing a sense of the limitations which confine those at home, is work indeed. To communicate such reporting effectively means having confidence and giving confidence, all at a time when, just as today, everything seems to be in flux and unstable.

At home in capitals, policymakers and advisers are not only vulnerable to the self-imposed pressures of a particular style, whether pragmatic or 'ethical', but also to a wider context of current outlook. The world weary nostrum that 'ultimately all politics are local' may strike a cynic as having a grim truth. But for the purposes of working across cultures and mindsets to resolve problems, the aphorism is unhelpful. It arrests the outreach and engagement necessary to reach resolutions which differing parties are willing to sustain. Paradoxically, it can obscure the urgent modern difficulty that what seems foreign can, in a globalizing world, soon make its way over to our own context and become an internal problem.

Huntingdon's *Clash of Civilizations*, published in 1996, undoubtedly caught the mood of the immediate aftermath of the Cold War and it gained great currency as a shorthand for understanding the muddle. Long-established patterns of behaviour around the world appeared to be breaking up. Islamist activists were beginning to catch the attention of non-specialists. The 'Afghan Arabs' returning from victory in Afghanistan made headlines for wider trends that were resonating with earlier worries about the Islamic revolution in Iran. They posed new security problems not only in the Middle East but outside it. The first attack on the Twin Towers in New York was in 1993. The troubled Balkans could be seen as a manifestation of ancient hostilities between Cyrillic Orthodox, Muslims and Latin Catholics. People reached out for these vivid descriptions which explained and which could be powerful in discussions among senior men grappling with unfamiliar and difficult issues.

As a base, however, on which to build a more detailed analysis and prescribe likelihoods, these descriptions were unreliable. So today expressions like 'The Shi'i Crescent' or 'The Arc of Instability' can tell us much about our own fears, but can get in the way of a more helpful external assessment. When reading foreign languages, we have to watch the endings of words, watch the detail of grammar. In thinking through policy questions, if we are to be relevant, we have to take some of the detail into account. Our own assumptions about what is significant may be misplaced. Our own political masters' confidence about what 'really matters to people', so important to their success at home, may, abroad, also be misplaced.

The Middle East imposes hard stresses on those who try to report on it and on those responsible for policy making. The fundamentals and incidentals are not so easily distinguished, especially against the short timeframes set for political reactions. Sudden events require a response. The 'foreseeable future' today may not be as much as a few years, and in that frame the deep, palpable currents of discontent or gathering trends may not have time to break open at the surface. The long view can be discarded as 'academic', 'theological' or, at worst, 'irrelevant' to the deadlines of the day. Just as we have to watch the endings in the grammatical sense, we have to keep an open mind about the temporal endings of dramas in which it seems easy to be decisive at the start, but which turn out to be more troublesome as they open up. Furthermore, much that concerns us in the Middle East, like security matters, is intentionally kept well away from the surface both by the local authorities and by those in opposition working against them. It is often hard to adduce or articulate evidence for what seem convincing judgements.

In the developing world, troubling trends or tensions may be clear, but the resilience of the population in putting up with difficulties and the determination of regimes to suppress trouble are way outside our own political and social experience. Both are extremely difficult to judge against a timeline. Countries can fester with maladministration, economic and demographic pressures for much longer than we would think possible. Regimes can summon up the willpower to inflict repressive measures, long after we have thought them running low on steam.

Religion and Politics in the Middle East

The high incidence of political turbulence, coups and revolutions gave the Middle East a wide reputation for instability in the twentieth century, and the reputation has stuck. Although many of the region's problems now derive from a lack of political movement, we remain on edge and expect difficulties, but we find it hard to know when matters will 'go live'. At the time the 'Arab Street' was much quoted by the Jeremiahs of the media during the run-up to both Iraqi wars, and with good reason, but 'the street' did not turn out before the fighting. Some regimes even felt free to stage popular demonstrations just to make tactical points to their local American embassies. They knew their own, and we did not. Once there was no regime in Iraq, of course things changed.

Our discussion of the politics of the Middle East is also cramped by our own sensitivities, and first among these is our diffidence in talking about what we call the political dimension of religion. An observer once commented that Islamist terrorism presented the United Kingdom with its gravest non-military threat since the Counter-Reformation. The terms of that remark may not be attractive, but they were presumably meant to capture the extraordinary determination of today's adversaries and, perhaps, the thought that the measures used to deal with the threat in history are not available to us now.

Religion in the Middle East has long been the idiom for discussing what in our terms are political interests, how people want to be governed. This is because secularization has not taken a deep hold in the Middle East, and because Islamic thought sees religion as the only trustworthy compass on which to navigate the problems of human life. The proper guidance and rule of the community is not allocated to some separate category of thought. Yet revelation and the utterances and practice of the Prophet, collected as Hadith, do not prescribe any particular form of government. So the debate is intense as people become frustrated with oppressive governments, whether revolutionary in origin or tied to the interests of a particular family which achieved ascendancy in pre-modern times and has managed to hold on to power.

There is a dynamic diversification of views going on in the Arab world and in the wider Islamic community. Our own labels of 'Islamists' and 'moderates', if they were ever useful, are no longer so. Debates about law and modernity, the role of shari'a, about the proper forms of government, from consultation (shura) to caliphate, about relating to existing governments, from participation through objection to rejection – all these and more teem in ferment in the Arabic press, on websites and conversation. The terms of these debates in a culture so mindful of its past are obscure to us, and vary greatly in the differing microcultures inside the broad Arab world. Arabs in the peninsula grapple with a heritage passed down by the Wahhabis, while Yemenis and some North Africans have trace elements of a Shiite past. While Egyptians deal with the tradition of the Muslim Brothers, Jordanians and Mesopotamians have to contend with disputes arising from the controversies over the role to be played by the descendants of the Prophet's family. And these are only some of the themes.

What does seem clear amid the hubbub (which is itself causing some anxiety to ordinary people, who wonder where all this upheaval will end) is a recurrent theme – 'how are we to relate to the West?' Gone is the idea that modernization and development necessarily mean westernization. The question then arises whether the assumption present in so much thinking about the processes of globalization, that convergence is inevitable, is right or wrong. At present, divergence seems more likely, as thinkers and religiously observant people in the Arab world determine that their engagement with outsiders be predicated on a refinement of practice which allows compliance with their own religious precepts.

This ideological and religious restlessness may be expressed in terms that appear internal to the local culture, but it is not happening in isolation. The impact of the West, or just the massive fact of its standing next door, as did Byzantium to the early Muslim community, promotes complications both in reaction and aspiration. Our own comments, never mind our military interventions, get into the current and colour it. When our assertions, like freedom being the deepest desire of all peoples, seem to miss the urgent hopes and agenda of people in the region, the people sense an indifference to their concerns and a separate set of objectives which may, or may not, align with their local interests. Religious commitment and identity may be reckoned to be fundamental interests in the Middle East and both attitudes have had centuries of practice in surviving oppressive government, not to mention, as they would wish us to point out, our own colonial activities.

Democracy and the Arabs

The absence of democracy in the region and its history has given the people a different experience from that sensation of loss we should have if our democracies were taken from us. The fact that 'democracy' in Arabic is a loan word lends a suspicion that the project lacks local authenticity and proposes a borrowed system of government that may not fit local circumstances and tradition. This is not to say that the people of the region are not interested in freedom, in participation and 'right governance'. The yearning for the experience of the 'rightly guided caliphs' (the four who immediately succeeded the Prophet, who were by no means oppressive) has become a commonplace. Our own holding up of democracy as a good way forward in political reform misreads the local sense of priorities. Our suggestion presupposes that there is agreement on the nature and extent of the community to which it could be applied. Just as religion causes us nervousness, so we are inhibited in considering the fundamental terms of identity in the Arab world. Nationality should by no means be taken as one of these.

We are not keen to open up discussion about a reworking of the state boundaries that were laid down early in the twentieth century. In the region, such an idea is likely to be taboo but only amongst elites tied to today's centres of power. The people of ancient centres, like Damascus or Mecca, draw a confidence of their own from their roots, quite unconnected with today's regimes and so, to a greater or lesser extent, with others. Identity is not wrapped in a flag, but comes from the deep well of genealogy, intermingled, depending on tradition, with religion or sect. These loyalties to blood are absolute and fundamental.

The position does not differ greatly in many regimes. Regimes too, for instance throughout the member states of the Gulf Co-operation Council, can be based on family. And a coup within a ruling family (no rarity) remains loyal to the blood. The scale of the family may be enormous, as in Saudi Arabia, but the bloodline is distinct, clear and, of course, exclusive. In so far as these regimes make sure that family interest and survival colours policy, so too do the people put their immediate family, clan or tribal interest firmly at the centre of their own outlook. This narrow dispensation of power imposes some detachment on the ruled. They have little access to power and lead their lives on a by-pass route that protects them from entanglements with the regime. In this sense, civic society that means so much to us, and which we should like to see as an amenity promoted in their national development, already has considerable reality and vigour. But it is built on personal connections woven across the institutions of families and clans, rather than the more formal associations and impersonal institutions that have grown up in our very different societies. In consequence, our assumptions about the common good or common interest in Middle Eastern states may not match the aspirations of the people living there.

When power is at issue, as in Iraq, control of space, policy and programme becomes the immediate priority for each community. The underlying geometry of society is exposed, and with it the frictions and feuds which the twentieth-century regimes were only able to cement over with their massive, centralized state power. As we watch developments in Iraq, the Lebanon, in Palestine and other countries, these fundamental issues are working, like long wavelength signals, through the chatter of day-to-day politics.

It has often been said that experts are nearly always wrong. It is true that learning is not the same as wisdom. Impatience with 'cultural factors' is reassuring when matters are coming to a head and hard decisions are to be taken. But those charged with high duties, like the formation of policy, can easily mistake the depth of their own wisdom. In other lands an opposed conviction may lie at an equal depth and well above the level of simple common humanity to which the policy-maker is appealing.

In our own societies, the extent of central government seems to be making it difficult for those high up to reach down in departments to obtain co-ordinated and coherent advice. The problem is evident in the proliferation of yet more political advisers. The vitality and effectiveness of our own institutions were part of the strength of our systems of government. They made provision, through their hierarchies, for the problem that experts might have little awareness of the operational pressures bearing down on those at the top. The experts' and researchers' contribution was included in the upward process of advice towards the top.

The pressures and threats in today's world and particularly in the Middle East tempt us to apply our performance culture to finding solutions. Something must be done and the progress towards it measured. Caution can seem unhelpful when there is so much to be done. Yet, as in foreign languages, we have to pay attention to the endings, fundamentally important features, even when they seem mere detail, or just features of a culture. Without them we run the risk of not making sense, of not being understood. Without them, like Job, after much to do and talking we have little but to listen to the voice from the whirlwind: 'Who is this who darkeneth counsel by words without knowledge?'

16

A TWENTY-FIRST-CENTURY
ENERGY POLICY

Branko Terzic

Mankind needs energy to exist. It always has. Demand for energy has always increased as populations have grown and as modern lifestyles have become more energy intensive. That trend of increasing energy demand and intensity continues into the twenty-first century. Up until recently finding sufficient supply at affordable prices to meet rising demand has been the main problem. Today that quest is complicated by the consensus of scientific opinion that humanity's prior energy conversion activities, relating to the burning of fossil fuels, have added excessive greenhouse gases to the atmosphere, and unless checked further activity will lead to catastrophic climate change effects. Thus we are faced today with the entwined problems of obtaining necessary energy supply while mitigating future greenhouse gas affects.

There are, however, lessons from the twentieth century in energy policy and regulation which can guide our decisions into the twenty-first century, and help us meet this dual challenge of meeting humanity's rising energy needs while preventing catastrophic climate change. The last century saw an unprecedented improvement in the quality of life through increased energy intensity while at the same time expanding the global population. In large part this progress was enabled by the engagement of market forces, availability of private capital, implementation of progressive governmental regulation and incentives for efficiency in production and use.

The evolution of energy use by humanity enabled the progress mankind has made in improvements in health and nutrition, lengthening the intellectual day, reducing or eliminating physical labour and allowing communication in numerous forms at the speed of light. Moving from horses to horsepower freed up a quarter or more of cultivated land for food production, but also resulted in energy intensity increases. As Alfred W. Crosby notes in *Children of the Sun*, 2006, use of primary energy increased 20 times since 1850 and five times since 1950 in the developed countries. In the last quarter century world energy demand has increased by 60%. The problem faced today is that world energy demand into the next quarter century is expected to more than double.

In practical terms the topic of 'energy' can be separated into two related areas – energy from oil for transportation (38% of world total), and energy from other sources (coal at 26%, natural gas at 23%, renewable at 7% and nuclear at 6%), mostly used for electricity production and space heating. Thus, today most of our primary energy comes from stored energy of the ancient sun in the form of fossil fuels. It was the conversion of energy from these fossil fuels that drove two of the major scientific and industrial developments in the twentieth century, namely mass production of automobiles and the electrification of much of the world.

As standards of living improve around the world the demand for energy will increase as, at the beginning of the twenty-first century, the lesser developed world improves its lifestyles and the third of humanity which still does not have access to delivered electricity strives to obtain even basic service.

In the past the transportation-fuel-providing oil industry and the electric power industry worlds moved in separate paths, each under its own unique set of circumstances. That may not be the case in the future. This is best exemplified by the 2007 report of the US National Petroleum Council (NPC), entitled *Hard Truths: Facing the Hard Truths About Energy*. The report was in response to President George Bush's 2005 letter requesting the NPC to study 'What does the future hold for oil and natural gas supply?' The response, however, addressed the broader issues of global electricity demand and fuel supplies. One reason for this broader response is the necessity to look ahead at the future role and growth of electric-powered vehicles. A transition to vehicles tied, for supply and possible delivery back, to the electric grid presents a myriad of new possibilities with respect to displacing significant quantities of oil as a transportation fuel, lowering greenhouse gas emissions and providing storage and distributed electric generation to the grid. The result of such a technology breakthrough would be a need for an integrated look at all forms of energy supply and demand.

Regardless of the form of fuel supply, it is my opinion that solutions to the problem of energy access at reasonable prices are to be found in our experience to date with prior successful oil, natural gas and electricity policies. The lessons of the twentieth century I believe reflect what we know about the operation of successful energy markets, the availability of private capital and the necessity of progressive governmental policies. The introduction of a new and alarming condition, the potential disastrous consequences of global climate change likely caused by humanities' conversion of energy to useful purposes, does not invalidate our previous experience. It becomes another consideration to which known solutions can be applied.

A survey of the literature on the subject of energy policy from such organizations as the World Energy Council and the World Bank finds common policy recommendations and themes based on a century of experience in the developed world. Among the most recognized of these themes are the following:

1. Energy markets can work well, if designed well.
2. Private capital is available at reasonable cost when governmental and regulatory policies are progressive.
3. A necessary pre-condition to obtaining energy resources and infrastructure at reasonable prices is the implementation of good governmental and regulatory policies based on well-established norms.

A new addition to these three components in the twenty-first century should be:

4. An emphasis on policies that provide the right incentives to efficiency, to moderate demand and decrease emissions all along the energy value chain.

The combination of these four themes will be the key to nationally and globally balancing future energy supply and demand while mitigating climate change effects.

Energy Markets

Reflecting back on twentieth-century energy policy, one can say with certainty that markets in energy can work all along the value chain. The most recent introduction of energy markets has been that of the expansion of wholesale markets for electricity in the United States from actions of individual states, and the requirements for both wholesale and retail access to competitive markets for both electricity and natural gas markets in the European Union.

In the case of wholesale and retail electricity markets, it is noted frequently that California's wholesale and retail markets failed at the beginning of the new century (2001 to 2002). At the same point in time, however, the larger Eastern US electricity market, the PJM Interconnection LLC, was working quite well. The California market was designed in the state and consisted of new state legislation and state regulatory components approved by the US Federal Energy Regulatory Commission. In retrospect it was clear that California's electricity market was poorly designed and badly regulated. The lesson of the California electricity market failure is that badly designed markets will, indeed, work badly. That other markets in the United States and Europe have worked provide lessons for policymakers. Among these lessons learned is that functioning wholesale power markets need to be established before there is any hope of retail market competition.

In the US's natural gas markets, regulation of natural gas production prices between 1950 and the 1980s by the Federal Power Commission and its successor the Federal Energy Regulatory Commission (FERC) resulted in shortages of natural gas interstate markets and sustained high prices. FERC's complex multi-tier pricing mechanism, federally mandated restrictions on natural gas use and complex orders on gas transportation and sales policies of pipelines could not cure the fundamental problem of government's inability to set prices correctly. Having proved that government was not good at regulating natural gas prices, Congress correctly deregulated natural gas prices at the well-head, resulting almost immediately in increases in natural gas supply and lower prices for consumers for the next two decades.

International crude oil markets are more complicated, but until recently most observers gave markets the credit for insuring adequate supply at reasonable prices. Clearly global oil markets worked well in times of surplus. Today's tight markets, with prices near $100, balance supply and demand, but carry premiums reflecting multiple risk factors, not all immediately understood or explainable by participants. The predominate longer term view holds that both OPEC producers and OECD consumers want adequate supply at reasonable prices without major disruption to the flow of oil in one direction or cash in the other. As a majority of drilling for oil and gas has occurred in the lower 48 states of the United States, it is expected that additional drilling activity worldwide will result in adequate new supply under most market pricing scenarios. A minority view holds to the idea that a 'peak' in oil production has or is about to occur, but real time events and new discoveries and extraction techniques keep pushing out the forecasted 'peak' dates.

Private Capital

Another lesson of the twentieth century is that adequate private capital is available, and has always been available, to build out our energy infrastructure. Much of the world's efficient infrastructure in pipelines, distribution networks and LNG facilities for natural gas and generation, and transmission and distribution facilities for electricity, have been financed by private capital and operated by investor owned companies.

Estimates of capital requirements for energy infrastructure vary greatly and depend on numerous assumptions. Near-term requirements include new generation and transmission to meet both demand growth and to replace existing worn-out facilities. Decisions concerning limitation of future greenhouse gas emission from existing power plants may accelerate the retirement of existing power generation units, requiring additional new electric production capacity to be built. Under all circumstances the costs of new units on a per-unit of energy produced basis will cause future prices to rise. Modest levels of inflation in construction costs, additional environmental considerations, scarcity of land and rights-of-way, and other factors, all portend higher installed plant costs than experienced in the past. Add to this the fact that in many locations existing rates are based on the depreciated cost of old units, and it is clear consumers will see higher costs even without the factoring in of higher fuel prices for coal, natural gas or uranium, the most likely fuel choices. Increasing amounts of renewable energy may reduce some demand for conventional fuels, but under today's scenarios even heavily subsidized wind and solar projects result in prices higher than for conventional fuel alternatives.

The good news is that, even under the closest governmental regulation of residual transmission and distribution monopolies, whenever market-derived returns were available capital has been plentiful for those facilities. This has been the positive result of capital attraction where regulatory risks are quantifiable and estimable. The lesson globally is that good regulatory laws, policies and ongoing progressive regulation have been necessary preconditions for capital availability at reasonable cost.

However, this regulation must follow and implement laws and policies which themselves must be clear, constructive and compatible. Successful government policies have come from the application of known economic principles that are not incompatible with transparent considerations of the 'national interest'. Neither is progressive government policy that attracts private capital incompatible with appropriate environmental considerations, parameters and mitigation.

Climate Change Considerations

Among environmental considerations in energy conversion is the newer and potentially catastrophic issue surrounding global climate change. The concern is about the potential for catastrophic climatic effects caused by emissions of greenhouse gases associated with energy production, conversion and end use. The logic is compelling. At this point in time it appears that industrially developed countries have filled most of the atmosphere's capacity to accept additional greenhouse gases. As a result many feel that the developed nations now have the moral imperative to restrict their own emissions to both make room for latecomers and to reduce future concentrations. Many argue that the US must lead in this effort, even if it is now no longer the world's single greatest polluter. The consequences of not doing so are dire.

At this point in time a majority of scientists, when it comes to the question of effects of greenhouse gases, say that the earth's capacity to absorb our mistakes (or ignorance) is limited. The scientific consensus, right or wrong, is that we now know enough to take actions. Of course, the actions to be taken should be measured and proportionate to our knowledge of the facts. Greenhouse gas emissions by sector from all sources are estimated by the World Resources Institute (2000) to include contributions of 24.5% from electricity and heat, 13.5% transport, 13.8% industry, 13.5% agriculture, 18.2% deforestation, 3.6% waste and 12.9% from other sources.

It is suggested that governments can 'phase in' their climate change responses in a manner which most effectively addresses the problem, minimizes the disruption and buys time with respect to evolving climate change knowledge and mitigation technology. The Stern Review describes four ways to reduce greenhouse gas emissions: (i) reducing demand for energy intensive goods and services, (ii) increasing efficiency, (iii) taking action on non-energy emissions (deforestation), and (iv) switching to lower carbon technologies for power, heat and transport. One way to approach the needed reductions is by sequencing actions in three phases or classes.

The first phase, or Class I, of actions would be those that are immediately practical and affordable. One major source of greenhouse gases is transportation fuel related – and that is where we should start with conservation steps, mass transit and improved fuel efficiency. Space heating and electricity production are also major greenhouse gas producers. Reductions in the use of electricity, through the introduction of efficiency measures and changes in the sources of electricity production, would significantly reduce greenhouse gas emissions.

These actions, especially steps taken to improve efficiency, also have immediate societal value. Improving efficiency lowers consumer spending, and produces long-term value to consumers by reducing the need for, or timing of, the introduction of expensive new power plants. In Class I actions we have practical solutions related to the more efficient use of energy, significantly reducing greenhouse gases while producing significant economic benefits for consumers. One does not need to even accept the theory or existence of the global climate change problem to see the benefits to consumers and society of energy efficiency improvements under the Class I classification.

Class II actions are those that might not be economic under current financial analysis today, but that deserve consideration, and maybe subsidy, because they bring related social benefits. Class II actions might include alternative energy and renewable fuels that require direct or indirect subsidies. Champions for this effort will often rally around the strategic benefit of 'energy independence' or 'energy security', plus local job creation. Carbon-dioxide trading schemes or a 'carbon tax' to reduce greenhouse gases fall into this classification as well. American policymakers should begin with Class I solutions immediately, but Class II actions should get some serious attention in the next phase.

Finally, Class III activities are those with some potentially valuable solutions to reducing greenhouse gas emissions, but are not economically easy to implement and do not have add-on social value. Class III actions we would consider are government mandates, programmes or restrictions that can reduce greenhouse gases, but also have anticipated side-effects such as reducing productivity, increasing prices of goods and services, decreasing national competitiveness and lowering national security. We may have to resort to more Draconian efforts, but it is not the place to begin.

Thus, among the first policies recommended for adoption, according to this scheme, would be those which support and advance 'energy efficiency' in its broadest sense and all along the value chain. This means regulatory policies that provide incentives for efficiency in acquisition of fuels and assets, conversion technologies and operations, transmission and distribution, and end use.

Regulation

Successful energy policies will require effective and progressive utility regulation, based on knowledge gained in almost 100 years of regulation of private capital financed energy infrastructure. Most of this experience has come from the United States, and more recently from the United Kingdom. Electricity and natural gas regulators have, in most cases, successfully balanced the requirements for insuring adequate services under 'just and reasonable rates' against the needs of investors to obtain 'fair return' (market derived) for invested capital. Good regulation can be a substitute for competition, and seeks to achieve the same ends including rewarding efficiency all along the regulated value chain and when achieved by the consumer.

Regulators must engage, where possible, the ability of markets to extract efficiency and then apply efficiency incentive programmes to companies under regulation. This means that adoption and application of performance-based regulatory schemes is fair and consistent. This form of regulation, best recognized as the United Kingdom's 'RPI-X' annual indexing scheme, explicitly allows the sharing of efficiency in electricity transmission and delivery services between shareholders and consumers.

Progressive regulation also means looking at proposals to allow electric and natural gas companies to make investments in demand-side programmes with the same regulatory treatment, for the same effect, as provided by regulators for supply-side investments. This notion of recognition of permanent demand reduction on the same basis as the addition of a megawatt of capacity, called by such visionaries as Emory Lovins a 'nega-watt', has now even gained support among a handful of utility executives in the United States.

Reducing demand for delivered electricity also means coupling the technology available in 'smart meters' and 'smart appliances' with 'smart tariffs' taking advantage of real time pricing opportunities. The first discussion of such real time pricing occurred after the first energy price shocks of the 1970s, but fell out of favour as prices dropped in the 1980s and 1990s. It's time to revisit these techniques.

Included in the regulator's smart tariff reform for electric and gas utilities should be the 'decoupling' of profitability in the monopoly services from volumetric sales. Recent recognition of the disincentives to consumer conservation and end-use efficiency by existing rate designs has been made by environmental groups such as the National Resources Defense Council in the United States. Such support has enabled a number of state regulatory agencies to reform rate designs, removing disincentives to regulated companies to support efficiency and conservation programmes.

Energy efficiency programmes undertaken by consumers under progressive regulatory and governmental policies provide multiple benefits. In reducing consumption, consumers reduce both immediate electric bills as well as future bills by delaying the construction of new, more expensive, energy production facilities. Lower electricity consumption also has the immediate and long-term effects of lowering any associated greenhouse gas emissions associated with electricity protection.

National education programmes can alert consumers to the fact that the consumer's monthly electric bill is affected by three factors – the consumer's own metered consumption, the maximum or peak demand and the prices charged. In developed countries electricity consumption is related to multiple factors including lifestyle choices, weather conditions and the efficiency of a home and its power-consuming equipment and appliances. Most consumers can lower their bills today with a combination of end-use efficiency programmes, improved weatherization and attention to their usage patterns. Few choose to do so. However, informational campaigns, leading by example and making 'energy efficiency' a profit centre for incumbent utilities, could dramatically change consumer behaviour for the better.

Summary

The twentieth century demonstrated that markets in energy can work, that private capital is available and that progressive regulation based on correct national policies is a precondition to success in providing adequate energy at reasonable prices. The new potential for climate change catastrophe recognized in the twenty-first century adds an additional reason to support programmes and policies that support and enable efficiency in energy conversion, transmission and consumption. While no silver bullet exists to address the multiple issues of balancing supply and demand and mitigating greenhouse gas emissions, there is a combination of policies that can do the job or buy society time until better solutions come along. Prior experience demonstrates that progressive public policies which engage market forces, treat private capital fairly and provide incentives to efficiency all along the energy conversion and usage path can supply a set of solutions to the energy and climate change dilemma of the twenty-first century.

17

THE NEW MIDDLE AGES

Simon Jenkins

Two years ago the Gleneagles 'awareness raising summit' cost £10m per delegate and pledged soaring aid to world poverty, as did the United Nations' previous millennium conference on the same subject, which reportedly drained New York of champagne and caviar. As a result, for the first time in ten years world aid has fallen. After Gleneagles everyone said they pledged an extra $50 billion only 'to be nice to Tony after 7/7', and did not mean it. Do politicians really think the public cannot see through the cynicism that passes for modern foreign policy?

Bush's undermining of the G8 by announcing his own climate change summit might be stalling tactics, but at least it called the G8's bluff. A summit of the 15 top polluters, summoned by the biggest of them all, is more likely to make progress than the G8 or the UN. Blair limbered up for his last extravaganza by touring the world in favour of 'liberal interventionism'. His final speech was made, appropriately, in South Africa where, at the height of the United Kingdom's imperial outreach in the Edwardian era, young men in Lord Milner's 'kindergarten' came to spread the Bible, western values and good government among the heathen.

British interventionism has evolved since Blair's scene-setting Chicago speech of April 1999. In Ethiopia in the 1980s nobody suggested using armed force to topple a government that was starving millions of its people to death, any more than force was used to stop Saddam Hussein's genocide in Kurdistan or that of the Indonesians in Timor. When the West sent soldiers to Lebanon and Somalia it retreated with a bloody nose. People did not like being invaded, for whatever reason. Only UN-approved wars to repel aggression, as in the Falklands and the Gulf, seemed to work.

The turning point was the arming of aid convoys in Bosnia in 1992 and the resulting mission creep. By the time that civil war had spread to Kosovo in 1998, the idea of bombing cities that offered no threat to the world seemed commonplace, as if the West had reverted to Guernica. The United States bombed Baghdad, the United Kingdom bombed Belgrade, Israel bombed Beirut, Russia bombed Grozny. Blair's innovation in Kosovo was to persuade Bill Clinton that such bombing was futile if not supported by a ground invasion. He was right, but from then on his blood was up.

In his Chicago speech Blair argued for 'a new generation of liberal humanitarian wars', going far beyond what was necessary for national defence or self-interest. He claimed the right to make the world a better place at the point of a gun. Even Henry Kissinger termed the speech 'irresponsible'. But it was not until after 9/11 that Blair converted what he had defined as humanitarian intervention into a global crusade, a war for 'values' and even for 'civilization'.

As Blair admits, he found foreign affairs more absorbing than domestic. Abroad he could talk of an 'international community that is overtly values based', without needing to say what it meant. He found war exciting, having never experienced it first-hand. He pleaded to bomb Kabul before the Americans. He loved chatting to generals, and wanted sand trays set up in No. 10 to watch operations. Liberal interventionism was no more than a verbal backdrop to what was 'feel-good with guns'. It answered those who accused Blair of being all mouth and no muscle.

The Prime Minister could plead two factors in support. The first was an undoubted public craving for 'something must be done' about cruelties long frozen by the Cold War and now publicized by the mass media. The invasion of Kosovo, although illegal, had such a humanitarian imperative. Secondly, internationally sponsored violence by Islamists found a widespread bond of grievance in Palestine. This posed a menace to some western (and eastern) cities, but in no way justified Blair equating it to a third world war. It was like treating the mafia as a threat to world capitalism. Blair's 'global war on terror' elevated random bands of criminals to the status of glorious warriors. He might parade as tough on terror, but he was anything but tough on its causes. His cackhanded Middle East diplomacy has left a region more unstable than when he took office.

Liberal interventionism talks the talk but can barely walk the length of a red carpet. It has failed the most crucial test of any policy, in being neither morally even-handed nor effective in action. Britons have been treated to the sickening sight of Blair shaking hands with Colonel Qadaffi of Libya and even selling him missiles. How does this madcap dictator, sponsor of terrorism and suppressor of his people, pass liberal muster? He had cobbled together some useless bits of tin, called it a nuclear programme and then offered to dismantle it if the West aided his wrecked economy and armed him. Blair and Bush fell for the most blatant con in modern diplomacy.

Where again is the moral content in the United Kingdom's dealing with the authoritarian rulers of Pakistan, China, Ethiopia and Saudi Arabia? When Blair says that the Sudan regime's actions in Darfur and Robert Mugabe's in Zimbabwe are 'unacceptable', what does he mean? As Kant demanded, a moral diktat applied to one must be applied universally or it is neither moral nor a deterrent. More seriously, Blair's policy has not worked. He has not withdrawn from a single one of the countries he has invaded – Sierra Leone, Kosovo, Iraq and Afghanistan. The reason is that he has not installed liberal values, merely invaded and occupied them.

The flagship interventions, Iraq and Afghanistan, have brought death, misery and instability. I cannot imagine a plague spot on earth that would swap its plight for that of 'liberally intervened' Basra or Baghdad. Meanwhile, the United Kingdom and the United States must go cap in hand to the dictators of Iran, Syria, Saudi Arabia and Pakistan to rescue their armies from defeat, a political as much as a military humiliation.

There is, or was, a valid recipe for intervention enshrined in the charter of the UN. Military aggression by one state against another (not just a criminal conspiracy by a group of citizens) should be resisted, by force if necessary. It was valid in Korea and Vietnam, and successful in the Falklands and Kuwait. Internal state repression, such as to prevent violent partition, is not normally the business of the outside world until it degenerates into humanitarian atrocity. This may, as in Kosovo, Sierra Leone or Rwanda, justify an attack. But it is most effectively met by the sticks and carrots of diplomacy and charitable relief – as is still the case in most of the world's trouble spots.

States remain sovereign entities, and must make their peace with themselves. As Iraq has shown, the scope for potent politico-military intervention is limited. The message of the past decade is surely that intervention should struggle to be non-military and non-governmental. Recently another five Britons were kidnapped in a country to which we claimed to bring freedom, justice and prosperity. Blair's response via the Americans was not to gather intelligence and seek allies in recovering the hostages. It was to smash into Sadr city in tanks and, when an inhabitant offered to open his door, blast a hole in his wall and beat him up. Such action must have made dozens of enemies and may have cost the lives of the hostages. Probably intended for television, it was utterly counterproductive. I can think of no better metaphor for the gangrene that afflicts British policy.

Insurgency and brutal repression are the normal outcomes of foreign occupation, as occupation is of invasion. For a decade in the 1990s the United Kingdom intervened at arm's length in Iraq, containing a dictator even if immiserating his people. The new interventionism finds this inadequate for the grandiosity of its leaders. In a reversion to the motivation of the Middle Ages, they must send their soldiers to fight and die for abstract nouns. What is outrageous is for Blair to claim for the liberal cause what has been random adventurism.

Afghanistan

To the British left, Afghanistan was always the 'good' war and Iraq the 'bad' one. It is permitted for ministers to assert that they were 'privately opposed' to Iraq, so long as Afghanistan is seen as a worthy cause. With the United Kingdom at its helm, Afghanistan would be all it was not under the Americans. It would make the United Kingdom look macho. It would revitalize the UN and NATO after perceived debacles in former Yugoslavia and it would fulfil the United Kingdom's historic role as nation-builder to the world.

Iraq is post-imperialism for fast learners, Afghanistan for slow ones. While the concept of a benign outcome in Iraq is strictly for armchair crazies, such an outcome remains received wisdom in Afghanistan. The British ambassador, Sir Sherard Cowper-Coles, is building himself an embassy to compare with the US's in Baghdad, and has forecast a British military presence of 30 years. Brigadier John Lorimer in Helmand says he can suppress insurgency in ten years, but will need 'longer than 30' to establish good governance. Such things were being said in Iraq until two years ago, when the body bags began to talk.

Kabul is a city awash with thousands of troops and aid workers from some 36 countries, all supposedly involved in 'security and reconstruction' and almost none able to leave the capital by land. A reputed 10,000 NGO staff have turned Kabul into Klondike during the goldrush, building office blocks, driving up rents, cruising about in armoured jeeps and spending stupefying sums of other people's money, essentially on themselves. They take orders only from some distant agency, but then the same goes for the American army, NATO, the UN, the EU and the supposedly sovereign Afghan government.

In the provinces, the Americans are running a guerrilla army out of Bagram, trying to kill as many 'Taliban' or 'al-Qaida' as possible, while the British heroically re-enact the Zulu wars down in Helmand. Neither takes any notice of President Hamid Karzai, whose deals with warlords, druglords, Iranians and Taliban collaborators are probably the best hope of stabilizing Afghanistan when the foreign occupation is over. But since that is claimed by the United Kingdom to be virtually never, the only certainty is a rising tempo of insurgency.

Over time in any occupation, the occupying force falls apart and its components fight for their own vested interests. Consider three policies now being pursued in Kabul. The first concerns drugs. There are 15 separate organizations devoting their time (and £200m of British money) to eradicating Afghanistan's one indigenous source of income, opium. In that time the opium harvest has broken every record, and trying to suppress it has alienated farmers and fuelled insurgency. Everyone in Kabul knows the policy is both stupid and counterproductive, but since grants and jobs are tied to it, the policy is entrenched and will not change.

Then there is the bombing of Pashtun villages for sheltering the Taliban. Thousands of civilians have died as a result, inducing hostility to occupying forces and a desire for revenge that recruits thousands to the cause of killing western troops. But soldiers sent to fight the Taliban have been ill-equipped and outgunned and needed air support, while air forces have craved a 'battlefield role'. Again, the policy is known to be counterproductive, yet continues because it delivers a cheaper 'kill rate' and satisfies military interests.

A third policy is the most overhyped in British military history, that of 'winning hearts and minds'. Not only is it meaningless without adequate security, which would require 50,000 rather than 5,000 troops in Helmand alone, it also involves tipping large sums of cash into nervous tribal villages, tearing apart power structures and creating feuds and dissension, the money usually ending up with warlords or the Taliban. All this is known in Kabul, but the money has been allotted and must be spent, however counterproductive the outcome.

In each of these cases, the mis-match between what makes sense and what is implemented is total. Kabul is already a monument to how vested interests can negate the best of interventionist intentions. Toppling foreign regimes is a dangerous and unpredictable business. But when invasion becomes occupation, freelance nation builders become freelance empire builders, each with budgets and jobs to protect.

Getting out of Basra is now a firm diktat of British defence planning. The only sensible question in Kabul is how long before the same diktat applies there. The longer it takes, the weaker the alliances engineered by Karzai over the past three years will become and the more certain his fall will be. The longer Whitehall thinks it can win a war against the Taliban, the more it risks tearing Pakistan apart and sucking Iran into the conflict, both of which would be completely daft. Yet that is where liberal intervention is now leading. It is a post-imperial spasm, a knee-jerk jingoism and plain dumb.

18

GLOBAL WARMING: IT'S CHINA (AND INDIA) AS WELL AS THE UNITED STATES

Simon Scott Plummer

Protection of the environment is *the* political issue of the new century. David Cameron has embraced it, most dramatically, by his visit to a glacier in the remote island of Spitzbergen. Gordon Brown has polished his green credentials by doubling air passenger duty – at the same time generating an estimated £1 billion in extra revenue. David Miliband, the former Environment Secretary and the current Foreign Secretary, sees tackling climate change as a moral cause with economic, social, cultural and security implications.

Conservatives and Labour are involved in a bidding war of greenery. Mr Cameron is proposing a fuel duty on domestic flights and a sliding scale of passenger duty to reflect the number of flights an individual has taken in any one year. Tony Blair and Mr Miliband launched a climate-change bill which set legally binding targets of a 60% reduction, from the 1990 figure, in carbon dioxide emissions by 2050.

At local level, the Liberal Democrat-controlled Richmond Council, backed by Ken Livingstone, the Mayor of London, is considering raising the cost of parking permits for gas-guzzling vehicles in the borough.

According to a survey of children between seven and 11, conducted by the supermarket chain Somerfield, half are worried about the effects of global warming, often losing sleep because of it. Harrowing images such as those of polar bears suffering because of the melting Arctic ice-cap will keep climate change high on the agenda. And despite the claims of some scientists that solar activity rather than carbon dioxide is responsible for global warming, politicians will continue to play on the public's sense of guilt to engineer, through fiscal measures, changes in the way we live.

However, in the domestic debate over buying cleaner cars, taking fewer flights or switching to low-carbon sources of power for our homes, we should not lose sight of the global context. The United Kingdom and its EU partners can have a significant, and exemplary, effect on the drive to reduce global levels of greenhouse gases, which include carbon dioxide, nitrous oxides and other gases emitted by industrial processes. But the main polluters are the United States and China. Unless they can be persuaded drastically to lower their emission levels, the overall outcome will be negative. That entails making the management of climate change a prime goal of foreign policy.

Favourable Conjunction

Fortunately, the present conjunction of events is favourable to a British leader who would take up that challenge. Across the Atlantic, as the Bush presidency limps to a close, the Democratic-controlled congress has introduced a series of bills addressing global warming. It is difficult to see the next occupant of the White House, whatever his or her political persuasion, treating the issue with the indifference shown by the present administration. At a meeting in Washington in February 2007, politicians from both the Group of Eight (the United Kingdom, Canada, France, Germany, Italy, Japan, Russia and the US) and from Brazil, China, India, Mexico and

South Africa agreed that developing as well as industrialized economies would have to meet targets for cutting greenhouse gas emissions. They also called for the formation of a global market to cap and trade such emissions, and for a successor to the Kyoto Protocol, which expires in 2012, to be in place by 2009.

The Washington meeting of the Global Legislators Organization for a Balanced Environment (Globe) was an informal affair whose decisions were not binding. But the inclusion of Brazil, China, India, Mexico and South Africa indicates a significant shift in developing world thinking on climate change. Put crudely, the previous attitude was that poor countries should not be penalized for a situation brought about largely by their rich counterparts. The Stern Review, which was commissioned by the British government, estimates that since 1850 the United States and Europe have produced about 70% of all CO_2 emissions due to energy production, while developing countries' share is under 25%. Now there is a realization, at least at the highest level, that rich and poor countries are in this together and must jointly tackle the challenge of stabilizing greenhouse gases in the atmosphere.

The Stern Review defines the problem as follows. Before the Industrial Revolution, the greenhouse gas level was equivalent to about 280 parts per million CO_2. The current figure is about 430 ppm. With the rise has come an increase of 0.5°C in the global temperature. If current trends continue, that could increase by a further 2–3°C over the next 50 years or so. The impact, in the form of both floods and desertification, will be felt first and most acutely by the poorest countries.

The annual cost of stabilizing the greenhouse gas concentration at 450 ppm CO_2e is estimated at 1% of gross domestic product by the middle of the century. Delaying action would add considerably to that total. 'Investments made in the next 10–20 years could lock in very high emissions for the next half-century, or present an opportunity to move the world onto a more sustainable path', the review concludes.

China and India

To appreciate the full extent of the challenge, one need look no further than China. Already by 1994, the first year for which it presented figures to the United Nations, it was second only to the United States as a greenhouse gas producer. Average annual growth of around 9% will have added significantly to the total since then. Indeed, it is estimated that China could overtake the United States as a polluter by 2020. The country's leaders are aware that they have an environmental disaster on their hands, whether through soil erosion, contaminated water or filthy air. In that respect, China is following other Asian countries which industrialized earlier. In the 1950s and 1960s Japan experienced the horror of Minamata and itai-itai diseases and of Yokkaichi asthma, while in the 1970s and 1980s the rapid growth of the South Korean economy led to heavy pollution of the Han River, which flows through the capital, Seoul.

What is different in China's case is that the economic transformation is on a vastly greater scale and, as yet, there is not sufficient political pressure from below, because of the lack of representative government, to counter its frightening effects. Take, for example, the Yellow River, considered to be the cradle of Chinese civilization. Today, what was known as 'China's sorrow' because of its propensity to flood is running dry through the demands made on it by agriculture, industry and residential development. The state of Huai River is even worse, its waters being judged too toxic for irrigation. As mentioned above, there is awareness at the highest level of government of this catastrophe. In 2002 China signed the Kyoto Protocol, although as a developing country it was not bound to meet specific targets for cutting emissions, and in 2004 it announced plans to generate 10% of its power from renewable sources by 2010. It has also undertaken to cut the energy used for each unit of gross domestic product by 20% between 2006 and 2010.

These are hopeful indications of change but against them must be set the country's hugely ambitious targets for further growth. That is likely to be largely fuelled by coal, which supplies about 75% of China's energy needs, and to be accompanied by a rapid increase in the number of automobiles. Both of them threaten to make a mockery of efforts elsewhere in the world to stabilize the concentration of greenhouse gases in the atmosphere.

A more deep-seated obstacle to cleaning up China is the weakness of the government. Post-Mao, the Communist Party's legitimacy derives from maintaining the conditions for rapid economic growth. It is likely, therefore, to be chary of adopting radical targets (speaking globally, the Stern Review mentions the need to reach more than 80% below the absolute level of current annual emissions) which might threaten that growth, and its ability to achieve even the more limited goals it has set must be open to doubt. The party's continuing monopoly of political power has led to corruption on such a scale that commands from on high are easily thwarted by a combination of cadres and businessmen at the local level. The latter can find their way around central government regulations by simply bribing the former. Climate change thus represents one of the biggest challenges to party authority since the founding of the People's Republic in 1949.

In India, which since independence in 1947 has been a democracy, the opportunity for grass-roots involvement in tackling global warming is much greater. The government has set out what it calls an Integrated Energy Policy for the period 2006–2010. Yet, like China, it is enjoying high rates of growth (an annual average of 8.6% over the past four years), which it will be loath to forfeit. A report commissioned by the Asian Development Bank concludes that carbon dioxide emissions from vehicles in India will rise 5.8 times over the next 25 years (the equivalent figure for China is 3.4 times).

The Task for Government

With stabilizing greenhouse gas concentration as a central plank of its domestic and foreign policy, the government should first strive to ensure that the United Kingdom's commitments under the Kyoto Protocol are met. There is no doubting the Labour Party's recognition of the importance of this issue but, as so often over the past decade, the achievements do not match the rhetoric. CO_2 emissions have risen since 1999 and the goal of cutting them by 12.5% from their 1990 levels will not be met.

Despite being the protocol's most enthusiastic supporter, the European Union as a whole is likewise failing to meet its targets. As one of the most important EU members, the United Kingdom could play an exemplary role both in keeping its partners up to the mark and in developing the Union's Emissions Trading Scheme as the nucleus of future global carbon markets. At the moment, the lead is being taken by Angela Merkel, the German Chancellor who is hoping that a post-Kyoto agreement will be able to reconcile the technology-driven American approach to fighting global warming with Europe's combination of mandatory emission limits and a carbon-trading system. At a summit in March, EU members agreed to cut carbon dioxide emissions by 20% from their 1990 levels by 2020, with the hint that that could be extended to 30% if the United States, China and India came on board. They also pledged themselves to a 20% increase in the use of renewable fuels by the same date.

The Stern Review concludes that 'stabilization of greenhouse gas concentrations in the atmosphere is feasible and consistent with continued growth'. That will require both switching to non-fossil fuels and, in cases like that of China, where coal is likely to remain an important source of energy, developing techniques of carbon capture and storage. The experience of the United Kingdom in this transformation could be of great help to the developing world. At the same time it promises to be commercially rewarding. Stern estimates that the market for low-carbon energy products is likely to be worth at least $500 billion by 2050.

The Group of Eight should examine the pattern of its imports from the developing countries to see how they can promote low-carbon growth. This is the most effective leverage that the outside world can have on an economy such as China's, which is heavily dependent on exports; its trade surplus with the United States alone is over $200 billion. At the same time, the practice of sending electronic waste to China and other parts of Asia for recycling and disposal should be carefully monitored. Because of lack of regulation in the recipient countries, this dumping is exposing them to even greater levels of toxicity than those they already produce domestically.

The United Kingdom's Global Reach

History has left the United Kingdom in a unique geo-political position. It is the US's closest ally. It is a leading member of the EU. It is connected to the English-speaking developing world through the Commonwealth. And it is a permanent member of the United Nations Security Council. These links make it ideally placed to influence global thinking on climate change, whether in persuading the United States to sign up to the successor of the Kyoto Protocol, in confronting China with the damage it is doing to its own and the wider environment by its exceptionally wasteful use of high-carbon energy, or in promoting carbon capture and storage within the EU.

That message will be all the more effective if the United Kingdom can lead by example, and persuade the rest of Europe to do the same. The danger is that political parties in this country will get bogged down in a pre-election Dutch auction over taxing air travel and gas-guzzling vehicles, or phasing out incandescent light bulbs, while neglecting the much greater challenges which lie across the Atlantic and in Asia.

In the ways suggested above, a Conservative government should shoulder responsibility for the global implications of climate change and use the unique position of this country to influence the outcome. It would be churlish not to recognize that the Labour Party has made a start down this road; witness the commissioning of the Stern Review and the setting of a legal framework for a low-carbon economy. But the way is open for the Conservatives to weld the various strands of public concern about environmental degradation into a coherent whole with a global perspective.

19

THE CHALLENGE OF THE TWENTY-FIRST CENTURY

Robert Harvey

The world at the dawn of the twenty-first century is entering a radically new era. Historically, the first half of the twentieth century could be defined as the clash between the largely European nation-states, and the second half the rivalry of the superpowers. The beginning of the twenty-first century represents the dominance, although by no means omnipotence (as we are seeing in Iraq and Afghanistan), of a single superpower, the United States, and the emergence of a handful of regional powers across the world – the biggest being the European Union (which is economically as powerful as the US, but militarily much weaker), Japan, Russia, China, India and Brazil.

It is also a world of so-called 'asymmetrical' terrorist challenges and rogue or failed states, taking advantage of the new ease of communications to export obscure local causes from thousands of miles away to sow sporadic terror at the heart of the post-industrial West. It is, too, a world in which the far more alarming issue of nuclear proliferation – the acquiring of nuclear weapons by unstable middle-sized powers which could conceivably supply them to terrorists – remains unresolved and provides probably the single biggest security threat of our times.

Reserves of finite resources such as oil and water are endangered by political upheaval and scarcity, and global warming has emerged as a huge concern for millions of people. The skewed effects of economic globalization have raised serious problems, and poverty remains a colossal challenge. To end on a brighter note, it is a world that has seen enormous strides in economic development over the past decade, with the prospect of economic growth further dramatically improving the lives of hundreds of millions of people.

In this unfamiliar landscape, governments have for the most part taken refuge in the familiar landmarks of the post-World War II era – the United Nations, NATO, the European Union, the International Monetary Fund and the World Bank, to name but a few institutions fashioned to meet the challenges of 50 years ago when two nuclear-armed superpowers faced each other. It is as though we preferred to keep to the lifeboats when they have already made landfall. It is time to call into being new institutions to redress the imbalances of the old (to paraphrase George Canning).

Later I will suggest ways in which these institutions might be adapted to cope with more localized, if no less lethal, challenges posed by rogue states, violators of human rights and terrorists. But it is worth first glancing at the principal issues that will face the United Kingdom over the next three years or a new US administration in 2009.

The Wider Middle East

Most immediate and obvious are Iraq and the wider Middle East. Iraq is self-evidently in the middle of a sectarian civil war, precipitated by the fall of Saddam Hussein's autocratic and barbarian regime at the hands of western coalition forces. There are no easy or bloodless ways out. If US and British forces stay they risk increasingly being trapped in the crossfire between Shiites and Sunnis, largely serving the interests of the former, whose government we are protecting in the name of democracy, against the latter. Withdrawal may worsen the civil war in the short term, which is why it is seen as 'responsible' not to advocate such a course. But if the conflict is worsening despite our best efforts, it is hard to see how western (in particular British) interests are served by our maintaining our current role.

There is a very real concern that the war will spill over into one embracing the whole Gulf region, with all the implications this has for oil supplies and the global economy. The biggest problem at the moment is Iran, whose ambitions to become the dominant power in the oil-rich Gulf have been hugely advanced by the invasion of Iraq and the fall of Iran's most dangerous enemy, Saddam. The Iranians are seeking to set up a buffer Shiite state in the south and centre of Iraq which would give them virtual hegemony over the Gulf oil producers and, under a Pax Iraniana, more than double Iran's oil reserves and output. With a population equal to that of all the Gulf oil producers put together, they are already dominant.

The Iranians are also seeking to acquire a nuclear capability that would quickly give them the ability to produce large numbers of nuclear weapons. It is absurd to view this prospect with equanimity, as some do. The regime in Iran is far from stable, is openly, militantly Islamic, proselytizes revolution, supports Islamic terrorists abroad unashamedly, and could one day supply them with nuclear material – a prospect which caused the French government recently to underline that a terrorist nuclear attack supported by Iran would be viewed as a nuclear attack by Iran itself and invite nuclear retaliation. Far worse, far from never being able to use nuclear weapons to real effect, Iran could indulge in nuclear blackmail towards this oil-rich region on a whole variety of issues, from oil prices to supporting Shiite irredentism in Saudi Arabia, Kuwait or Bahrain, to territorial claims, navigation rights etc.

The immediate response of the regional neighbours to a nuclear Iran will be to seek to develop their own (avowedly peaceful) nuclear capacity, as Saudi Arabia, Egypt, Turkey and even Kuwait are already threatening (Israel would certainly expand its own nuclear arsenal). The Middle East is not a region in which the prospect of several unstable Islamic regimes confronting each other with nuclear weapons can be viewed with anything other than huge alarm – and our children will not forgive us if we failed to do all that we could to resolve the threat before it became unstoppable.

No responsible British government can rule out supporting military force to check or delay Iran's nuclear progress if the US judges this to be necessary. (An Israeli strike would be deeply undesirable, as it would serve to radicalize much Arab opinion onto Iran's side, whereas Arab opinion is currently deeply hostile to the traditional Persian foe.) But before then peaceful options should be exhausted, although not to the point of allowing Iran to acquire nuclear weaponry. In particular a full package of incentives such as US-Iranian diplomatic recognition, full access to the western economy, and western expertise to help develop gas and oil fields should be offered in exchange for Iran's shelving the nuclear option. There is a precedent for dealing with unsavoury regimes like that of the mullahs – witness President Nixon's China visit and policy of détente with the Soviet Union. In addition, Iran needs to be dissuaded from further meddling in Iraq through the offer of such links, but also backed up by the threat that the West will help Iran's own minorities, such as the Kurds and the Sunni Arabs, if necessary. A two-track approach of firmness and the offer of friendship is required.

Apart from the nuclear issue and the need to prevent Iranian domination of the Gulf, the most dangerous problem is posed by the possibility of the sectarian war in Iraq widening into proxy confrontation between Shiite Iran – for a millennium the hated Persian foes of the Arabs – and Sunni Saudi Arabia and other Gulf states, as well as Syria, Jordan and

Egypt. It is obviously in the West's interests to support its Arab allies against Persian expansionism, and thus effectively to change sides from the Shiites to protecting the Sunni minority in Iraq, but this also gives leverage with Iran. Do the Iranians really want to take on the Sunni Arab countries backed up by the resources and support of the West? (It might be argued that Russia and China would support Iran, but while those countries are to some extent cynically exploiting the Iranian crisis for their own ends, both face enormous Islamic challenges on their own borders and the emergence of an expansionist, nuclear-armed Iran cannot be in their interests.) It is to be hoped that Iran will shrink back from such a confrontation, being satisfied with its recent gains in the region. If not, it is in the UK's and the US's interests to support its allied Arab allies diplomatically and perhaps with money and arms, although not with troops.

On the issue of Saudi Arabia's long-term stability, the United Kingdom's links with the country should allow it to encourage that country towards a more reformist course, within its own traditions; but it would be counterproductive to proselytize and lecture loudly in public. In Egypt, as in Jordan, societies should be encouraged to put down democratic roots, but without crude external pressure. In Syria the answer is not 'regime change' of the kind that could put the Muslim Brotherhood in power, as is contemplated by some US policymakers, but pressure for a broadening of the base of the regime and above all for a settlement of the Golan Heights issue with Israel. There has long been every prospect of such an agreement. The Israelis have conceded that the Heights are not essential to national security, and the Syrians should be prepared to cease their support for Israel's enemies in exchange.

On the seemingly unending issue of Israel–Palestine, the United Kingdom must return to its traditional even-handed approach and abandon the pro-Israeli tilt of the Blair administration. The cornerstone of the United Kingdom's policy has long been Resolution 242 and the establishment of a Palestinian state based on the legitimate right of Palestinians to the occupied territories. In exchange the Israelis must have the security guarantees they require; a US peacekeeping force may be the only guarantee that both sides will respect. The outgoing Bush administration or its successor would be wise to restore this issue to the priority it deserves, and permit the Israeli-Arab reconciliation that would allow both to face the more dangerous threats of Islamic militancy and Persian expansionism.

Nuclear Proliferation

Moving from the Middle East to the wider issue of nuclear proliferation, the near fatalism of many about the effectiveness of the NPT regime is completely misplaced. True, North Korea, Pakistan, India and Israel have acquired nuclear weapons in defiance of the NPT, over nearly five long decades. But four other nations who had acquired them or were on the brink of doing so – Argentina, Brazil, South Africa and now Libya – have renounced them. It does not follow that because some countries have slipped through the net of international safeguards the net should be thrown away and everyone allowed to acquire them; instead the holes must be repaired to prevent an extremely dangerous and wasteful multiple nuclear arms race starting. Both the US and Russia could give a lead by reducing their own still unnecessarily high stockpiles of nuclear weapons.

On the issue of North Korea, we are dealing with the unique problem of an obscurantist and ruthless regime in a region that has made huge strides towards development and democracy in recent years. North Korea does not at the moment pose a threat of aggression against its neighbours; best to allow the latter to take the lead in seeking to defuse this inactivated time bomb. Economic incentives, rather than threats, would seem necessary towards even this evil little regime to avert a catastrophic and unnecessary war in the Korean peninsula. The February 2007 breakthrough in the six-party talks is hugely to be welcomed.

China

In the wider world the security challenges posed by the rise of China's economy have been overstated, and are probably containable through diplomacy and sensitivity. With the collapse of China's communist mission and its replacement by a more pragmatic view of the world geared to economic development, China represents more of an opportunity than a threat. However, there remain huge sources of political tension within the country, in particular the disparity of development between the rich coastal provinces and the impoverished interior, as well as the country's continuing lack of democracy and appalling human rights record. The Chinese armed forces still have a disproportionate influence, leading to occasional sabre rattling with Taiwan. There is, too, a new nationalism among young people that sometimes views the United States in particular with unreserved hostility.

The most dangerous issue arising from China's new nationalism is the return of its traditional rivalry with Japan, which expressed itself a couple of years ago in fierce anti-Japanese rioting. This admittedly is partly Japan's fault, as it has viewed China's economic rise with apprehension, even as it has invested heavily there, and has not refrained from provocative displays of nationalism at home. It is to be hoped that the pragmatic if uninspiring leadership in China and Japan will defuse tensions.

China's 'superpower' rise should not be overstated either. It remains an overwhelmingly poor country with a huge population and a low per capita income, and although its growth over the past decade has been spectacular, this is based on a shaky financial system, a still very inefficient state-dominated industrial structure and an environmental disaster in the making. Sandwiched between two great Asian powers, Japan and India (although for the moment it enjoys fairly friendly relations with Russia), and with the might of the United States across the Pacific, it is plainly not in China's economic interest to act as a regional bully – barring some unexpected internal convulsion.

Russia

Russia's re-emergence as a much-reduced regional bully under President Vladimir Putin's quasi-authoritarian nationalist regime poses serious problems for the West and has even caused talk about a new Cold War. NATO's continued expansion eastward after the end of the Cold War, as well as disappointment with the Russian's free-market economic experiment, appears to have resulted in a more nationalist mood, a return to a centralized economy largely funded by rising oil prices, and the end of the country's flirtation with western-style capitalism. Russia's nuclear stockpiles and armed forces remain huge. But clearly Russia will not present the same threat as it did before its loss of Eastern Europe and many of its southern republics. Rather, it has a considerable nuisance value in international diplomacy in respect of, for example, Iran.

The EU has a potentially major role in preventing any re-emergence of US–Russian rivalry. Germany's Chancellor, Angela Merkel, is directly engaging this issue, and the wisest long-term approach to Russia may be to consider its association or admission to the EU when and if its political climate becomes less authoritarian. Meanwhile, the United Kingdom and the EU should continue to press for greater democratic accountability. The United Kingdom's relations with the EU, the EU's with the US and the EU's own development, are discussed elsewhere in this book.

Energy

The issues posed by energy shortages and the related issue of global warming will take up an increasing amount of the time of any incoming British Foreign Secretary or US Secretary of State. It is hard to accept the current fashion for believing that climate change is the single most dangerous issue facing the globe today. Other challenges, for example those posed in Iraq and by Iran, North Korea and nuclear proliferation, are clearly more threatening. Nor, pace the recent UN report, is the scientific community unanimous in its attitude to what is causing global warming. But accepting that the bulk of opinion and evidence suggests that this is a serious medium-term challenge, it seems necessary to look for ways of reducing carbon emissions, possibly through a regime of worldwide carbon taxation, and seeking alternative fuels and technology and energy conservation. However, the main alternative technologies – wind power, wave power and solar power – are hugely expensive and at best intermittent and very partial solutions, while the capacity for hydro-electric projects is finite (and like wind power they are themselves environmentally damaging). Biofuels are also expensive. Nuclear power is dangerous and raises serious safety concerns, particularly in an age of terrorism.

The choices are thus not as simple as the eco-enthusiasts see them. An efficient international agreement needs to be much broader than Kyoto, and include firm commitments by the newly industrializing countries, in particular China and India (see the article on page 219 by Simon Scott Plummer), before the US can reasonably be expected to sign up to it. The United States is the principal importer of China's finished goods, and has much greater leverage with China on this subject than it realizes.

To those who argue that these countries need to enjoy the industrialization the West has enjoyed for so long without being penalized for the environmental cost, the answer should be brisk. The environmental damage done to their own societies by helter-skelter, carbon-fuelled industrialization is already huge, and they need to bring these problems under control to produce societies fit for their own people to live in. Are pollution-emitting satanic mills and mine disasters really the only alternative to rural poverty, or has the world learnt a few lessons some 250 years after the United Kingdom's own industrial revolution began the transformation? Energy saving and more efficient cars and reductions in smoggy emissions are as necessary in China and India as in the United States.

The issue of diminishing oil reserves, to which this problem is often linked, is similarly not as simple or acute as some believe. The problem largely results from a combination of political pressures and interference, and the way the world oil market works. Politically, oil is now largely in the hands of national governments which have manipulated the OPEC oil cartel in their own interests, seeking artificially high prices by playing up Middle Eastern political instability, Venezuela's nationalism etc. The oil-producing nations have also often done substantial damage to their own economies.

The real problem has been serious underinvestment in exploration, supply and refining capacity owing to the relatively low price of oil until a couple of years ago. In fact, most petroleum geologists believe there to be vast potential global sources of oil, such as Saudi Arabia's huge unexplored interior outside the eastern oil-producing region, southern Iraq, polar regions now being uncovered ironically enough by the shrinking polar ice cap or the (expensive to produce) bitumen tar reserves in the Orinoco basin and in Canada. The problem is not a shortage of oil, but of exploration or making oil cleaner – which may be technically possible. The more serious shortage may be that of fresh water in certain regions where competition for access may grow more intense.

Globalization

On the issue of globalization and global poverty, which itself gives rise to another major challenge in the unprecedented growth in migration from poorer to richer nations, the British approach ought not to be public relations offensives with unrealizable goals, like Gordon Brown's campaign to educate all of the world's people (even the British Empire had more modest aims), but a firm commitment to free-market and development policies that are actually pulling hundreds of millions out of poverty in India, China and elsewhere.

The problem is not that there is too much globalization but that there is too little of it, distributed in relatively small pockets while hundreds of millions of others remain mired in traditional poverty in the countryside and in slums. We need to spread the benefits of globalization, while certainly making the terms of trade fairer for the developing world and, through for example micro-finance initiatives, developing many more small-scale capital markets. In Asia the model of economic development needs to be more balanced, socially and geographically, as also in Latin America and Africa. This is not to be achieved by crude redistribution, which removes incentives, but through anti-corruption drives in Asia, greater political stability and regional integration in Latin America (as is already occurring) and, in Africa, the necessary vast improvement in traditional styles of government.

The challenge of the twenty-first century is enormously exciting for a whole new generation. It requires the recognition and addressing of new global problems using the tried and trusted foreign policy maxims of a balance of power, skilful diplomacy with force as a very last resort, acting in our national interests which include the promotion of British-style democracy, human rights and civilized values, and tempering our idealism with a strong dose of feet-on-the-ground realism.

Changing Institutions

What of the institutional challenge facing the United States specifically after Iraq? The US as dominant world superpower must engage more fully in the world in its own interests, as well as that of the planet as a whole. The two building blocks it has at its disposal – NATO and the United Nations – are seriously flawed. At present, the UN provides legitimization for police action by the world community and brings together the whole global community in a debating forum, however ineffectual, while NATO provides a (today highly cumbersome) framework for taking international military action against a country which transgresses the international order.

It does not require a genius to see how these two functions, authorization and implementation, might be brought together into a new global framework, with both the authority to act and the ability to implement its decisions. To do this requires some surgery on both organizations and, in NATO's case, probably even a change of name and formal dissolution of the alliance, retaining its core structures while allowing an entirely new structure to be built upon it.

Specifically, the new order must be based on an understanding of the following:

Firstly, that underpinning global security is the world's megapower, the United States.

While some countries might be unwilling to acknowledge this publicly, it is the central truth of the global condition at the beginning of the twenty-first century – the United States is the cornerstone, the guarantor, the shield. Others like Napoleon and Hitler have dreamt of such power. The United States is more powerful than any empire has ever been, and there is no discernible challenger. Napoleon's dream lasted just 15 years, Hitler's 1,000-year Reich barely a decade. The United States has been the world's most powerful country for more than 60 years, and its unchallenged master for nearly two decades. Only its democratic, constitutional and benevolent nature and, sometimes, its indifference to the outside world constrain it.

Possessed of the sole effective nuclear arsenal, a satellite surveillance system which will soon extend in detail to every corner of the world, armed forces that can arrive en masse to any world trouble-spot, the most technologically advanced aircraft, tanks and weaponry and a massive industrial base, the United States can do much of what it chooses. The reality of American power will not go away, whatever the wishful thinking of others. If in any global conflict the Americans were to turn the full extent of their industrial might on an enemy, as in World War II but with an economy 100 times as strong, heaven help its opponent.

While I would strongly argue that it is in the US's interests to defuse global tensions, I have no doubt who would win in any showdown. The key lies in persuading the US of the benefits of a particular course, not in believing that the US can ever be overcome. Any global security structure must recognize this reality, and be thankful that the US is such a benevolent megapower.

This established, the US now has to take a hold on itself. It is no longer enough for the world's megapower to make foreign policy by the seat of its pants, in an ad hoc, occasional manner determined by which party is in power or the considerations of mid-term elections. The disaster in Iraq conclusively proves that its own security, as well as that of the globe, is too important for that. President and Congress, Democrats and Republicans, politicians and public have a duty to resolve a new foreign policy consensus to fit the twenty-first century of the kind worked out at the end of World War II, and one which learns from the successes and mistakes of the following half century.

The neo-isolationism of the Clinton years and the erratic shoot-from-the-hip interventionism of the Bush years needs to be replaced with a more measured approach, involving at least three elements: a declaration of willingness to work in partnership with the rest of the world, preferably through representative regional groupings of nation-states; a determination to extend and enforce international law throughout the globe; and a readiness to take the lead in backing up this new global outreach with force or the threat of force only if necessary and on a fair and systematic basis. In addition, the ideal of spreading democracy and freedom throughout the globe must not be abandoned, while accepting that this cannot be done overnight. The first requirement of leadership is to treat other people as equals, even where this is obviously not the case, in an effort to secure their support and co-operation. This might be called the partnership concept.

The Clinton-era idea of the United States as an oasis of tranquillity in a troubled world, with the luxury of looking after its own interests while watching war, strife and poverty from afar, was brutally and definitively shattered on September 11. The concept of the United States as sheriff, doing its own thing against global bandits while cowardly bystanders watch, is so transparently childish that it is remarkable that it merits serious attention. Even old-style sheriffs needed deputies and posses; anyway, who frames the laws? And who looks after the other side of town while the sheriff is away?

The idea of American empire, so favoured by neo-conservatives, is not just ridiculous but dangerous. It is not true. The United States has huge economic and latent military power, but it cannot occupy large parts of the globe in the modern world. That is why the old European empires collapsed. Iraq proves that. It is also immoral. The United States has no right to dictate to the world on any issues save those of respect for legality, peace, human rights and democracy, which are universal. And it is heavily counterproductive, inviting other nations to assemble against it in the long run.

What is required is a much more modern concept – senior partner, chairman of the board, head of a grown-up family. The point is that the system and objectives of global law enforcement should be agreed by nine-tenths of the global community, and the actual enforcement should be accomplished by as many of these as possible, while acknowledging that the United States will sometimes be at the head of the troops. The global Wild West or jungle of paranoid neoconservative thinking in the United States, populated by rogue states, terrorists, criminals and law-breakers, is a myth. Nine-tenths of the globe is peaceful, and 99.9% of peoples would wish it to be so. They will respect the United States if it acts on their behalf as well as its own.

Secondly, the US's relationship with its allies in Europe and Japan is of critical importance.

This may not seem obvious at a time of endless transatlantic bickering, as well as the distinctly tepid reception Washington has accorded the European monetary union. There are even those who foresee Europe emerging as the US's chief rival in the next century. Japan, too, has long been regarded with ambivalence by the Americans.

Certainly trade rivalry and competition for third markets will continue, and may intensify. And certainly there is backbiting from the Americans on the one hand about Europe's failure to contribute more to global security (coupled with intense criticism whenever Europe tries to take the initiative), and on the other from the Europeans about the US's 'Wild West' diplomacy. But it is absurd to talk of hostility between the two when they have so much in common in dealing with wider and far more serious global challenges beyond. Both are bound by a common democracy, a common heritage and a common economic system. Both share the same values of respect for the individual and interest in upholding global peace.

What is required is a much greater tolerance on both sides – a respect for the US's economic vigour from the Europeans, and a respect for Europe's growing togetherness and efforts to find a voice in global affairs from the Americans. The European Union should not be seen as dangerous by the Americans. Rather, it should be seen as a partner and ally. Seeking to fragment the Union and divide and rule Europe is no longer an option for the United States, and its most far-sighted foreign-policy practitioners know it.

Far better for the US's own national interests is to be able to look to the European Union as a partner in exercising joint global responsibilities. If the Americans encourage Europe's foreign policy and global role, they will have less of a burden of policing the world and much greater influence with the Europeans. A long way down the line an 'Atlantic Union' between the United States and the European Union is in prospect, creating a common market between Nafta and the EU – something only possible between equal economic powers. Similarly the creation of the Euro is a force for currency stability, not for rivalry with the dollar. Co-operation between the two great currencies can only be good for global prosperity. If Russia eventually qualifies for EU entry, this axis of developed responsible powers will be strengthened.

The cultural, political and economic differences between the United States and Europe, and Japan, are somewhat wider, as are the divergences in strategic interests. Here again, though, it is in the US's interest to retain mature Japan as its principal ally in an Asian region fraught with potential conflicts and competing economic interests between immature, newly emergent middle-sized powers. Not least, it is in the US's interests to retain a special relationship with Japan to prevent the country ever re-adopting its former foreign policy course of national self-assertion.

The 'alliance of good' for global stability must thus be the United States, Europe and Japan, with Russia as a candidate member. For all its strength, the US's burden as sole global megapower will become intolerable unless it is shared with its European and Asian partners.

Thirdly, a 'northern alliance' must be evident that is not seen as exclusionary or hostile towards the four-fifths of humanity outside it.

However difficult this may be to sell to Congress or special lobbies, the United States, in its own interests, must seek to reach across the abyss of distrust that separates it and its north-ern allies from the non-European-descended nations of the world. The United States is uniquely well placed for this. In addition to being a European nation, it is an African nation, a Latino nation, an Asian nation and a Middle Eastern nation. Precisely because of its overwhelming power it cannot afford to attract the mistrust of the rest of the world; its efforts to win friends should be redoubled. There are many ways to do this. The United States and its northern allies should reach out to Islam with its more than one billion followers, engaging moderate Islamic countries in a dialogue at summit level alter-nately on their territory and on United States territory at least once a year.

Regional leaders such as Brazil, Mexico, South Africa, Nigeria, Egypt, Saudi Arabia (and one day Iran and Iraq), India, China, Indonesia, South Korea, Taiwan and Australia should also be engaged in a continuous dialogue, as should regional economic and security groupings. A much higher level of better targeted economic aid needs to be assembled in a 'development offensive' to widen the still all-too-narrow oases of economic development in the third world. However much this goes against the grain, the United States must re-engage – while seeking to reform – the UN, as this is still the main forum for consultation between the developed and developing world.

The fourth point to understand is that the UN must be a reflection of the reality of the world today, not as it was half a century ago.

Ideally the Security Council would be chaired by the US or the EU as global superpowers, although politically this is prob-ably impossible. What is not impossible is a Security Council that reflects the real division of power in the world – in fact one made up of the second tier of world powers after the United States, specifically Japan, Germany, France, the United Kingdom, Italy and Canada (G7), as well as Russia, China, Brazil, Egypt, South Africa, India and Australia (regional leaders). The principle of rotating membership for other countries on the Security Council should be retained.

The principle of the veto would ideally be abolished, although this may prove to be politically impossible, in which case the five countries that are its permanent members (the United States, Russia, the United Kingdom, France and China) should retain it. Otherwise a simple majority of the permanent members should suffice to authorize international intervention. In this 14-man directorate it will be seen that the western countries have a majority, but then so do smaller countries outside the NATO area. In addition, there would be five non-white members compared with just one at present.

Internationally, any military action would ideally be authorized by the widest possible consensus. Four out of five recent major military interventions – the Gulf, Bosnia, Kosovo (probably) and Afghanistan – would have secured overwhelming support from such a council (probably unanimous in the last two instances). Iraq would not.

The fifth item to be acknowledged is that NATO should be renamed the Alliance for Peace (AP).

This would be divided into two components – its core countries, and its member states. Core countries would today consist of the United States, Canada, the United Kingdom, France, Germany, Italy and Spain. Russia and Turkey might also one day be allowed to join. Global military intervention would require the consent of the core countries. Each of these would assemble a substantial force of volunteers from their own armies (say 20,000 each) to form a Peace Army for secondment to UN-authorized interventions as and when the necessity arose. These forces would be the elites of their own armies or private professional forces and remain based in the mother countries as part of their structures until called upon for intervention, but exercised to prepare them for joining an AP command. Additional regional forces could be used depending on the extent of the emergency.

The ordinary, non-core membership of the new NATO, the Alliance for Peace, would be extended, and include countries from across the world. The conditions for membership would be a willingness to participate, subscription to the major international organizations and peace treaties (for example, the Non-Proliferation Treaty), and constitutional democratic government respecting the rule of law and the rights of its citizens. Ordinary AP members could provide volunteer forces, in particular on a regional basis, for the Peace Army if they so wished; but they would not have the say to authorize intervention (other than to refuse to join in a particular intervention).

By limiting the Peace Army to just six or possibly seven or eight core countries, the new organization would be much more operationally effective than the cumbersome existing alliance, and would obviate the clumsy need for the United States to get so many of its allies on board, which manifested itself after September 11. Of course only as many members of even the core group as were necessary – in practice the US would decide – need actually take part.

By widening its membership to all supporters of international order across the world, the AP would have far greater legitimacy than NATO currently enjoys as just a rich man's club. By establishing the concept of (usually) all-volunteer forces as well as internationalism, armed intervention would be possible with much less of the morbid obsession that domestic media and publics have for 'body bags' – the fear of casualties incurred in foreign wars. By placing authorization for the use of Peace Army forces under the control of the expanded UN Security Council, such interventions would no longer be the actions of one nation acting alone or with one or more of its allies, but authorized by a UN council acting in the name of the whole global community.

It is important to emphasize that the new structure would not – could not – preclude acts by a country in defence of its own interests. The purpose of the structure would be to provide global legitimization for justified interventions around the globe, and the means to bring participants in such interventions together in an effective common structure. But if, for example, the United States chose to act alone to enforce an action which it saw as essential to its security (as it did in Panama or Grenada, for example) or if the United Kingdom did so (as, for example, occurred in the Falklands), provided that this was legitimized, there would be nothing to stop either country.

The next point should be that the new structure would work in conjunction with a series of local security alliances, with the aim of engaging the most powerful countries in each region.

These would embrace South and Central America, North Africa, sub-Saharan Africa, Central Europe, the Middle East, South West Asia including the former Soviet republics, the subcontinent, South East Asia and Australasia and East Asia. Such security alliances would provide for an early warning mechanism to determine the onset of approaching crises, as well as a mandatory arbitration procedure to resolve disputes between member states.

Those refusing to take part – possibly because they fear a judgement against them – would lose the advantages of membership. In other words they would not be consulted on regional issues, or even on those affecting their own security. The United States and other core AP members with direct interests in the area concerned would also be members of the regional security alliance and might, although not necessarily, take part in arbitration, policing or intervention. Typically, any intervention decided upon by the Security Council would seek the support of the regional security alliance members and their participation (where this was not a matter of local sensitivity) in the intervention force.

Finally, a key component of the new global security structure would be the early warning system for impending regional crises.

Member states and UN missions would have a duty to report potentially threatening situations or build-ups in their regions to a secretariat answering closely to the Security Council, so that these could be brought to international arbitration. This is intended to avert future Bosnias, Rwandas and Darfurs before they happen (not that the international community was unaware of these looming situations, but there was no statutory duty to offer any response). Countries refusing to co-operate or accept the results of arbitration would run the risk of UN-sponsored global intervention against them.

While such intervention would not be automatic – rigidity is as dangerous as it is unworkable in international systems – and each instance would be decided on a case-by-case basis by the Security Council (taking into account its feasibility, the seriousness of the violation, the likely duration of the commitment etc.), a last course of action would be effective military intervention authorized by the world community. This step-by-step and predictable approach to potential global flash-points is in marked contrast to the current state of uncertainty surrounding each international dispute. Equally, situations like the current absence of a serious dialogue between India and Pakistan over Kashmir, or between China and Taiwan, would become things of the past. These would have to be discussed at regional forums and, if tension escalated, arbitrated upon. Again, a state that refused to talk or abide by arbitration would put itself in the wrong.

This seven-point charter would bring together the current jumble of unilateral American-led military enforcement, multilateral bodies and the UN and NATO into a single global architecture, with clearly defined procedures and roles for all countries, as well as realistic provision for mediation and enforcement. To the immense majority of countries outside the immediate 'loop' of the United States and its closest allies, it would bring huge reassurance. The United States would address their immediate concerns directly in partnership in the context of their own regional security organizations; military interventions would take place as and when authorized by the UN through the enlarged Security Council, which would include a regional head, and would be debated by the General Assembly; and every country that qualified would have the right to be a member of the Peace Alliance, the military alliance and implementing branch of the UN.

Engaging the World

There will be those in the United States who argue, why bother with additional structures and bureaucracy? The reply must be that if the current unilateralism of American global policy is allowed to continue, the country will find itself not just alone in a sea of enemies but witness to flare-ups across the world that will be very costly to stop, disrupting its trade, inflicting serious damage on its interests abroad and resulting in September 11-style strikes.

Obviously the United States would survive such attacks and inconveniences, but why undergo them at all? Friendlessness is not an option in an increasingly integrated world. The danger for the United States is not isolationism – that is impossible today, and the consequences of such a policy were brutally evident even as far back as 1941 – but isolation. The world will respect a global system that it has shaped and which it feels it is part of, however much it might object to individual decisions, but it will increasingly contest an order which is enforced arbitrarily and unpredictably by a self-appointed sheriff who it believes is often acting merely in his own interests.

A framework for a new global order, the flattering offer of partnership by the United States to all countries that respect that order, co-operation in regional security organizations, consultation and friendship – these are the hallmarks of the global leadership that the United States finds itself the first country in history ever to be in a position to practise, an awesome responsibility. They are also the hallmarks of the democratic, open, multi-ethnic society that is the United States.

Unilateralism, the imposition of solutions, lack of consultation, capriciousness, naked self-interest, defensiveness in its dealings with friends, and edgy aggressiveness in its dealings with adversaries – these are the characteristics of an arrogant imperial power wielding military muscle, which is however limited if unable to persuade others of the righteousness of its cause. The megapower would certainly prevail, but as a global imperialist. This would be profoundly unworthy of a great nation founded on the three ideals of liberty, the rule of law and a fair deal for all, and unworthy of a people characterized by generosity and friendship. In the very long run such an approach is doomed, as empires have been throughout their history – as no country knows better than the United States, conceived in opposition to empire. If it treats the rest of the world as potential enemies they will become so in reality, and eventually coalitions will form that will challenge the United States.

Instead, in the position of global military dominance without competition that the United States finds itself in today, it has a unique opportunity to fashion an entirely new role for itself, one unprecedented in human history – that of benevolent head of the family of nations, settling disputes through negotiation and conciliation rather than force, commanding the affection and respect such a role deserves, and with an indefinite tenure at the head of the table for as long as both survive.

The United States has frittered away the past decade and a half celebrating its new status as uncontested world megapower (just as it took six years of chaos after independence for the United States to formulate a constitution). The next decade should be spent putting into place the relationship that will allow it to enjoy benevolent dominance for decades to come, or it will find itself to be a continent surrounded by a hostile, anarchic and possibly war-torn world which it will not be allowed to ignore (the lessons of September 11 and Iraq). The US's best use of megapowerdom is to share it.

Disengagement is not an option, but the United States can choose to engage the world on its terms and to shape the international agenda; or it will have to engage when events are largely beyond its control, at times and places of its enemies' choosing. The choice is between the United States against the world or a United States with the world, in which the US accords the same respect to other countries that it does to its own citizens drawn from so many other lands. That, truly, would be a worthy goal.